# Activity- versus Variability-Based Management Accounting

Poul Israelsen

# Activity- versus Variability-Based Management Accounting

A characterization and evaluation
of Activity-Based Costing,
based on the Variability Accounting System

Including some reformulations
of both systems

Jurist- og Økonomforbundets Forlag
DJØF Publishing, Copenhagen, Denmark
1993

*Activity- versus Variability-Based Management Accounting*
By Poul Israelsen
First edition 1993



DJØF PUBLISHING is a company of the
Association of Danish Lawyers and Economists



Cover design: Morten Højmark
Based on an idea by Mette Israelsen

Printed in Denmark 1993
by Narayana Press, Gylling

ISBN 87-574-6931-8

# Preface

Following the discussion of direct costing, the field of managerial accounting has been relatively stagnant for several decades. Only after the introduction of activity-based costing scholarly discussion in the USA has become lively again. This observation is not entirely true for Europe, because due to the contribution of Riebel in Germany and Madsen in Denmark some changes emerged much earlier.

The development of variability costing in Scandinavia based on Riebel's ideas of hierarchical structuring of cost allocation has initiated a much more detailed analysis of fixed cost and their relationship to various business activities; this, in turn, permitted a better in-depth analysis. Particularly the contributions of Madsen enhanced this approach. He placed added emphasis on the initial recording of cost in terms of their relationship to production factors, departments and cost objectives, as well as comprehensive non-monetary quantitative utilization information. However, he abstained from recommending immediate cost allocations, thus permitting later rearrangement of cost for specific analytic and decision purposes; this approach provides for a reduction of arbitrarily allocated amounts of overhead cost. His system forms a statistical addendum to any traditional accounting-based costing. He identified variability factors as common quantitative factors, with which cost – either automatically or through management disposition – vary almost proportionately. Thus he introduced a concept which is similar to current notions of cost drivers. The multidimensional analytic capabilities inherent in such a system – easily accomplished with available database software – provide the basis of Poul Israelsen's approach, which substantially advances current ideas both in academic and operational terms.

The author starts with a comparison of concepts underlying variability costing (developed and framed as a basic in-depth cost recording system) and activity-costing (designed as a product cost calculation system); then he summarizes their similarity in the cost objective – that is output dimension – , and their differences with respect to the cost accumulation at the departmental level, which always has been subject to a more detailed analysis in continental Europe. Variability costing provides for an unambiguous measurement of the resource consumption/cost relationships due to its hierarchical structure, a feature which exists only at a more aggregate level in activity costing. He specifically identifies the weakness of activity costing with respect to its dependence on actual capacity utilization – or simplified ex-ante assumptions – with relatively little transparency. He demonstrates, that variability costing not only permits more flexibility with respect to allocation of costs to various objectives and the analysis of stepped (sometimes) overlapping contribution margins. This increases the suitability of a variability costing system for the application of opportunity cost in strategic decision analysis situations, because existing historical records facilitate empirical identification of past cost dependencies in sufficient detail, namely at the lowest level of the hierarchy at which it was observable. As a consequence of an enlarged data input basis variability costing is not restricted to the two-stage allocation used in activity costing (activities, then cost drivers), although it can perform these simpler tasks.

Israelsen then compares the ABC costing concepts with Porter's activities and his postulated cost drivers within a value chain. For strategic cost analysis Porter suggests the potential existence of up to 10 drivers and recommends allocation of total costs including fixed items; this, again, raises the issue of unused capacity not fully adressed in ABC systems, because segments within the value chain are predetermined – whereas in strategic analysis these are subject to joint discretionary changes. Again variability costing creates an improved potential for analysis, because it provides the necessary information inputs without having allocated these overhead items beforehand.

Cooper and Kaplan in their more recent publications attempt to establish profit priorities within the framework of ABC systems by separating product-sustaining, batch and unit level allocations of 'expenses' – a cause-effect relationship. This moves the ABC approach one step closer to variability costing. However, this type of allocation is different from Madsen's 'stepped' contribution analysis, because he employs a finality relationship. In examining these differences Israelsen identifies the existence of different cost allocation hierarchies, namely (1) pure decision-informational stepped contribution hierarchies, (2) stepped contribution margin hierarchies, (3) tiered contribution analysis and (4) 'inspiration' analysis, which permits all kinds of additional ad-hoc allocation of relevant cost. From this vantage point he examines the advantages and shortcomings of various types of allocations for sales price determination. This task, of course, is dependent on the underlying production situation which calls for ex-ante ABC-like cost calculation in order to avoid preferences for long run unprofitable sales segments and a constant cost monitoring to permit selection or appropriate pricing for orders of varying sizes. Since not all data are needed at all times and required information inputs can be defined – or hypothesized – it becomes feasible to develop cost calculation patterns by identifying relevant borderline situations. These are developed and analyzed in the last part of this book. To accomplish this task the author integrates both his findings from the analysis of variability and ABC costing.

Israelsen succeeds in providing a penetrating in-depth analysis of both variability and ABC costing systems through comparison of their salient features and their shortcomings. His original arguments provide insights, which have not appeared anywhere before in the costing literature. They are derived from an intimate knowledge of both systems and strongly underline the effectiveness of international systems comparisons – because otherwise it might have taken longer to arrive at these insights. Even if a reader does not always agree with some of the conclusions, much better insights into the conceptual foundations of both systems and the need for their combination emerge from Israelsen's approach. This in itself represents an advance of scholarly discussions and understanding of presently unresolved costing issues. This book substantially contributes toward progress in management accounting and will form the basis for further developments in our field. It has been a long time that such a concise and comprehensive analysis was made available to readers.

January 1993

Dipl.Kfm. Dr. rer.pol. habil.
Hanns Martin W. Schoenfeld
H.T. Scovill Professor of Accountancy
University of Illinois at Urbana-Champaign
Illinois, USA

# Author's preface

My interest in Activity-Based Costing goes back to a conference I attended in Chicago, 1989, entitled "World-Class Controllership – Heading towards year 2000", arranged jointly by the US National Association of Accountants and The Society of Managements Accountants of Canada. Activity-based Costing was an important topic of discussion at this conference. Most of the participants were North American practitioners of and consultants in controlling, who saw in ABC a solution to many of the controller's problems. I became interested, and decided to take a closer look from a theoretical and methodological point of view.

Since ABC theory contains conceptualizations which are reminiscent of variability accounting terminology – not least the Cost Driver concept – it seemed only natural to use variability accounting ideas as a frame of reference.

Some parts of the book – in particular, parts of chapters 1 and 2 – had already been written in article form in 1990, but I delayed publishing them so as to be able to take account of the latest changes of direction within ABC.

I would like to take this opportunity of thanking the institutions and individuals who have made the realization of this book possible. I would like to thank The Aarhus School of Business – and Aalborg University before them – for granting me a senior fellowship. Thanks to Hanne Nørreklit and Lennart Nørreklit for their valuable and unstinting help throughout the whole process. Thanks also to Knud Rasmussen, who read the manuscript and gave many invaluable comments. I would also like to thank Poul Erik Sørensen for his joint authorship of an article which further stimulated my interest in this field. Thanks also to my other colleagues at the Centre of Economic Management for many useful discussions. I would like to give a special thanks to professor Hanns Martin Schoenfeld, University of Illinois at Urbana-Champaign, for his generous and constructive comments on the content and presentation of the manuscript, in addition to his help with its publication. Last, but not least, a thankyou to my translator, Steve Churchill, without whose professionalism and wholehearted cooperation this book would never have appeared in English.

Poul Israelsen
Nr. Sundby, January 1993

# Contents

# List of Figures

# 0. Introduction

*Activity-Based Costing* (ABC) has aroused a great deal of interest among both theoreticians and practitioners in recent years, especially in the USA. The aim of this book is to characterize and evaluate this costing system from the vantage point of variability accounting, a system widely used throughout Scandinavia. The reason variability accounting has been chosen as the frame of reference is because the similarity of terminology between this system and the ABC system. This applies to both the original version of the ABC system, in which the concept of the "Cost Driver" was introduced, and, more strikingly, to recent developments in the ABC world, in which great importance has been attached to hierarchy considerations in the description of costs.

Chapter 1 briefly introduces the fundamental features of the variability accounting system. This involves some changes and differences of interpretation and clarification compared with professor Vagn Madsen's original version. The exact nature of these differences is discussed in chapter 1.1.

Chapter 2 introduces and analyses the principles of a cost-accounting system based on the ideas contained in ABC. The starting point here – in chapter 2.1 – is Robin Cooper's five design choices for an ABC system.[1] It is described how these design choices and their respective tasks are solved within the framework of variability accounting. The analysis leads, in chapter 2.2, to an outline of a problem complex surrounding the recording depth of production batch costs, which illustrates that calculations in the ABC system are dependent on actual capacity utilization. This outline is also the rationale for pointing out, in chapter 2.3, that, as a basis for decision-making, the non-arbitrary recording principles enshrined in variability accounting do not automatically guard against arbitrariness, and the chapter closes with an introduction to the difference between problem-determined hierarchies and

1. In an instructive 4-article series in the Journal of Cost Management for the Manufacturing Industry, professor Robin Cooper describes the background, purpose, and consequences of using "Activity-Based Costing". The five design choices referred to appear in the last article, entitled "The Rise of Activity-Based Costing – Part Four: What Do Activity-Based Cost Systems Look Like?", *Journal of Cost Management*, Spring 1989.

natural cost hierarchies. In chapter 2.4 the scope of costs contained in the ABC system is explained and discussed, while the basis for the evaluation of costs is investigated in chapter 2.4.1 under the heading consumption costs versus opportunity costs. Chapter 2.5 presents a summary of the similarities and differences between the two systems, and it is argued how the ABC-idea – in its basic philosophy – can serve as a useful tool for identifying profitable and problematic sales segments, as well as a very suitable supplement to the policy control of costs used in variability budgeting.

Chapter 3 takes a closer look at the idea of Cost Drivers by going back to its inception in Porter's theory for the creation of competitive advantage,[2] where the concepts "Activities", "Value-chains", and "Cost Drivers" play a prominent part in the generated model. In particular, it is investigated whether Porter's driver concept is a rival or a complement to its use in the ABC system.

Chapter 4 discusses the new direction within ABC, in which its application as a product-cost calculation principle supporting external price determination is played down in favour of a more broadly-based profitability analysis of different sales segments. Cost hierarchies are an essential element in this type of analysis. The cost hierarchy used here is shown to be a hybrid, however, not to be confused with the North European models, including variability accounting hierarchies. It is demonstrated how the hierarchy considerations in the latest version of the ABC system – here called Activity-Based Profitability Analysis – are carried out within a variability context, and the discussion on natural versus problem-determined hierarchies is reopened to demonstrate the difference between the two, and to prove that the incorporation of natural cost hierarchies in a basic system of accounts will lead to loss of information unless one makes sure that these hierarchies are genuinely natural.

In the closing chapter – chapter 5 – the original justification for ABC, in terms of a differentiated product cost calculation for external pricing purposes, is reexamined. It is evaluated which type of companies has an interest in differentiated product cost at the ex ante stage. For the type of company identified, which is a manufacturer of custom-made products in varying order sizes, it is demonstrated how the original ABC system can be used to construct a tactical calculation-monitoring system, though not as an instrument for pricing decisions. For the latter, an operational ex ante calculation system is developed and described, combining the use of both consumption and opportunity costs, and resulting in an economically rational and practicable channeling of sales orders.

2. Michael Porter: *Competitive Advantage*.

# 1. Fundamental Features of the Variability Accounting System

The variability accounting system was developed by professor Vagn Madsen, University of Aarhus, in the 1950s,[3] as a replacement for the typical cost accounts – such as job-order or process costing systems, implemented either as full-cost or variable costing systems – which were (and still are) prevalent at the time. In Vagn Madsen's opinion, these systems could not be used as a general basis for a firm's cost accounts, inasmuch as they each aimed at solving only *one* of the tasks of cost accounts, viz. accounting profit, product calculation, control, and non-routine tasks. Dealing with the specifically chosen main task of one system complicates consideration of the other purposes, however, on account of the requisite – but task-specific – allocation bases.

Vagn Madsen therefore introduced a new primary purpose of cost accounts, which he designated the *cost-recording task*. The aim of this was to enable the cost-account records to be used for solving all the other accounting tasks. This occurs *outside* the cost accounts themselves, however, though based on their (among others) primary and rudimentary information. Variability accounting thus represents a very rigorous distinction between a data-*recording* task and a data-*manipulation* task. For this reason, variability accounting can also be characterized as a *multi-purpose* cost-accounting system.

If the recordings are not derived from the data needs of each individual calculation task, how, then, should cost recording be organised? On this point, variability accounting starts with the fact that any cost – at the moment of consumption – is characterized by the *type* of production factor consumed or used, the *department* in which it takes place, and the immediate *objective* for the use of this resource. This can be illustrated as follows:

3. Vagn Madsen, *Bidrag til Belysning af Rationaliseringsproblemerne i Industrivirksomheder*, Copenhagen, 1951, and later refined in *Regnskabsvæsenets opgaver og problemer*, first edition, 1959.

**Figure 1:** Dimensions in the cost recordings of the variability accounting system.

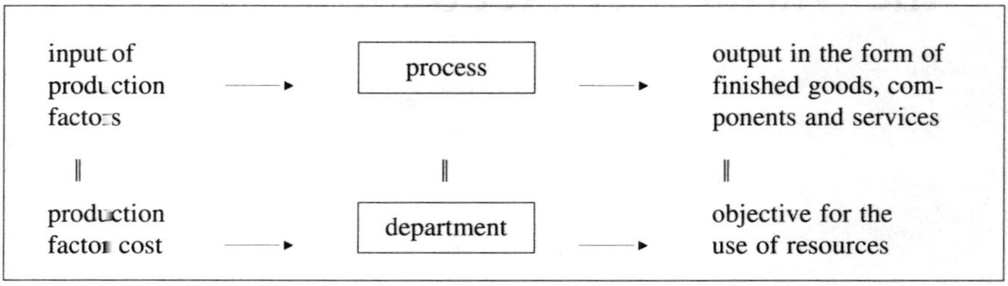


Thus any cost consumption recorded in the variability accounting system is simultaneously characterized by the type, department, and objective in such a way as to retain cross-referencing between the dimensions. In database terminology, an individual record contains an identification of each of the three dimensions:

**Figure 2:** The basic content of a record in the variability accounting system.

| 1 | 2 | 3 | 4 | 5 |
|---|---|---|---|---|
| Type of production factor | Department | Cost Objective | Quantity of production factor | Cost |

The first four cells of such a record constitute the basic registrations of the firm's factor input statistics (measured in physical quantities consumed or time used), whereas sections 1-3, and 5 are basic records in the firm's cost accounts. The factor input statistics form the basis of the cost accounts, and there is a close connection between these statistics and the cost accounts.

In the future, when computers become even faster than today, the record in figure 2 will, in an elaborate relational database system of accounts, become a so-called "virtual record" in a "virtual table" – what is often termed a "view" in the database language. This means that the table do not form part of the system's defined tables. Here, we will find a table describing the "factor input statistics" and an input-price table, the latter containing the price for each of the production factors. Since the relevant cost-valuation method depends on the analysis problem at hand, the price table might include a variety of prices – e.g. historical prices, current prices, standard prices, price-functions, and even opportunity costs. Multiplying the quantities in the factor-input-statistics table with a specifically chosen price from the price table gives us the specific cost figures in column 5, figure 2. Today, however, the cost valuation method used in variability accounting is *actual consumption at standard prices.*

Inasmuch as any resource consumption is characterized by each of the three dimensions, it can also be said for each recording period (accounting period) that the sum of the costs recorded as production factor costs is equal to the sum recorded as department-costs, which again are equal to the total cost consumption recorded under cost-objectives.[4]

Which factors affect the type of production factor costs, department costs, and cost objectives used in the variability accounting system?

If we look at the department and objectives dimensions first, there are three considerations: (i) the need to avoid and exclude arbitrary allocations in the cost account records, (ii) the desire to obtain as much informative data as possible, and (iii) the cost of obtaining information.

Arbitrary allocations can be precluded in both dimensions by constructing a hierarchy of accounts, consisting of superjacent, subjacent, and adjacent accounts. In the department dimension these accounts reveal the firm's organisational structure, while in the objectives dimension they reflect the tasks at hand, which are called "objectives for the use of resources" (equal to "cost objectives" or simply "objectives" for short) in the variability accounting system. As far as the product-manufacturing objective is concerned, this means a structured reflection of the firm's component- and finished products programme, with in-house components[5] at the lowest level, through finished products and groups of finished products, to "product manufacturing objectives en bloc" at the highest level. The objectives dimension of the account structure – outside the framework of the "product-manufacturing objective", though adjacent to it – includes a large number of other objectives, e.g. "maintenance objectives" (possibly subdivided into, for example, building and machine maintenance), "distribution objectives", "advertising objectives", etc.. For further examples of adjacent departments and objectives, see supplement 1, which includes Vagn Madsen's example of an account structure. It should be pointed out that this was only meant as an example by Vagn Madsen, since it

4. The fact that Vagn Madsen later (*Budgettering*, Copenhagen, 1970) divided the objectives dimension up into two disjunctive subsets – "operating objectives" and "investment objectives" – is ignored here, inasmuch as its prime importance is in presenting the profit and loss statement. For an example of what the investment objectives include, see the figure note in supplement 1.
5. Components purchased from outside suppliers show up as a "production factor cost" at the moment of consumption of the component.

is precisely characteristic of the system that the specification of each of the three recording dimensions are unique to every firm.

The principle for recording resource consumption in the department and objectives dimensions is that it is placed as far down the hierarchy as a non-arbitrary assignment allows, and for which a *measurement* of the actual resource consumption and/or use has been carried out. This principle implies that it is *direct* consumption which is recorded. If the cost consumption is indirect for two or more departments or two or more objectives respectively (i.e. common to them), then the cost item will be placed at the level immediately above the departments and objectives concerned in which case it becomes direct.

It can be seen, therefore, that variability accounting operates with a distinction between direct/indirect costs, but by relativizing the classification object (department, cost objective) for which cost consumption is recorded, the concept of "indirect" costs is invalidated as a cost-recording concept. In other words, in the variability accounting system, all costs are recorded as direct costs – both department- and objectives costs. From this, it can be seen that the fixed v variable cost dichotomy – as used in a direct variable costing system – is not employed. Such a dichotomy would namely require deciding and determining which tasks and planning perspective the accounting records should be used for, and this would conflict with the pluralistic nature of the system.

The information potential in the department and objectives dimensions' cost records depends on the degree of detail in their accounts structure. (We ignore here the potentially greater number of conscious and unconscious recording errors which result from the more detailed structure). For both hierarchies, the less depth – i.e. the fewer the levels – the greater the number of costs recorded in the higher-level account. Similarly, a limited breadth – i.e. a small number of adjacent accounts – implies that more costs "have to be pushed up the hierarchy". The data, and with them the potency of the information which can be extracted from the cost accounts, consequently become more limited. On the other hand, the accounting system can also be expected to be cheaper to set up and operate. It is in this respect that considerations of information cost are especially relevant.

Considerations of information cost are also pertinent to the next characteristic of variability accounting we shall be looking at, namely the question of selection and measurement of *variability factors*, about which Vagn Madsen says:

> "Apart from fixed costs,[6] each cost has its own direct quantitative factors with which it varies proportionately. Recording every single factor would be highly impracticable, however. The costs must therefore be systematized and joined into larger groups, each characterized by a common factor with which they vary approximately proportionately. These factors are called variability factors."[7]

Here, those costs which vary with the variability factor in question include both costs which vary automatically with the volume of output and costs which can be made to vary dispositively with volume. In relation to figure 1 above, the choice of variability factor means that, for each established cost objective, we have to identify, measure, and record a unit of output to which the costs of the objective concerned vary approximately proportionately. As regards the product-manufacturing objective, for example, it means recording the number of components and finished products produced. If the chart of accounts of the product-manufacturing objective also specifies batch costs, then here the variability factor can be "number of batches" or "number of direct hours used in setups". Examples of other variability factors outside the product-manufacturing objective are "number of kilometres", "number of ton-kilometres", etc., for the transport objective, and "number of TV minutes", "number of column inches", and "number of exhibition days", etc., for the advertising objective.

It can be seen, therefore, that a more thorough specification of the accounts structure in the objectives dimension not only demands more measurements and recordings to take account of the resource consumption of a larger number of objectives, but also the identification and measurement of a larger number of variability factors. However, in any consideration of information cost, the potentially greater value of information must be set against rising costs of measurement and recording.

The type of input of real goods and services is described in the *production factor cost* dimension of the variability accounting system. A large number of these also appear as expenditure items in the financial accounts, but it must be emphasized that, in variability accounting, it is the *consumption and use* of these resources which is recorded. Depreciation and interest fall outside this definition of "real goods and services", and are not included in variability accounts, which means that these items are exclusively dealt with in the financial accounts. Other production factors than externally supplied ones show up in the system of variability accounts presented here. This is the case

6. Here, fixed costs comprise depreciations only.
7. Vagn Madsen, *Regnskabsvæsenets opgaver og problemer*, p. 133. My translation from Danish. All non-English quotations translated by this author.

for all in-house components, which implies that all these components appear in the type of production factor dimension (when used as input) as well as in the objectives dimension (when produced as output). When used as input, however, they are not costed but only recorded in physical quantities, since the costing process has already taken place when the components were produced, i.e. when the component appeared as a cost objective in the objectives dimension. (See, in addition, footnote 8 and Appendix A).

In variability accounting, recording takes place solely in *statistical form*, and not according to the double-entry bookkeeping principle. This suggests that there is a dualistic connection between the financial accounts and the variability accounts, i.e. recordings in the two systems take place independently of each other, but in such a way that they can be balanced. One consequence of the statistical recording form is that, for each individual account in the objectives hierarchy, only the *extra* costs associated with the additional processing are recorded. The costs consumed in the preceding stages have already been recorded in subjacent accounts, of course.

Together, the statistical form of recording and hierarchical construction of the objectives structure imply that, when asked what costs we can save by discontinuing the production of an objective, we can only say – i.e. without further processing of the variability accounting data outside the accounts – that we save (automatically or dispositively) those cost recorded for the relevant objective, plus all the subjacent objectives of this objective, plus some part of superjacent objectives.[8] The limited nature of this reply is due to the fact that variability accounting contains only rudimentary recordings of cost consumption, without the use of allocation bases – i.e. without arbitrary allocations.

8. The superjacent objectives also contain costs consumed in the production of components/intermediate products which are used in several finished goods (or higher-level – i.e. more processed – in-house manufactured components). Such common components can be described as "multifunctional components". Placing the multifunctional component as a subjacent objective for each of the finished products is out of the question since at the time of production we do not know which finished product's subjacent objective to enter the component's costs against. The multifunctional component's objective account is therefore placed at a level in the hierarchy which has all the products in which the component is used as subjacent accounts. When the multifunctional component is later used in the production of a finished product (or more elaborate components), the quantitative consumption of the component is recorded in the finished product's objectives account, *but no cost evaluation of this consumption is carried out at this point*. This occurs only in connection with analyses which are extraneous to the accounts, inasmuch as the valuation depends on the nature of the problem being analysed. For a more detailed discussion of the intricacies of this problem, see Israelsen: "Lader Vagn Madsens og Zakken Worres tanker og ideer om virksomhedens omkostningsregnskab sig forene?"

The pluralism of the accounting system suggests that there are no automatic or built-in solutions to the various accounting tasks.

A summary of the characteristics of the variability accounting system is provided at the end of this chapter and an example of the basic structure of the system is given in Appendix A.

Interestingly, the recording dimensions of variability accounting are essentially those sought by A.J. Nanni *et al.* in a prize winning article in the Journal of Management Accounting.[9] In this, they state that a cost accounting system must be able to answer the following questions:

> "(a) How much was spent?, (b) Who spent it? (i.e. under whose responsibility or authority was it spent?), (c) For what purpose was it spent?, and (d) What results were obtained?"

As can be seen, the type of production factor dimension is not named explicitly, but elements of it appear elsewhere in the authors' article.[10]

As far as point (d) is concerned, the result or the effect of the resource consumption on a number of objectives can be described quantitatively, and thus form part of statistical records, which are coordinated with descriptions of cost accounts. In such a case, the descriptions of quantitative effects function as variability factors. This is typically true for a number of objectives in the lower region of the hierarchy, especially if, at the same time, they are peculiar to specific departments (e.g. departments' efforts to reduce the number of products and components which fall short of required quality standards). On the other hand, the effect of a number of other objectives – typically higher-level and interdepartmental objectives, and aggregations of objectives extracted from the basic recording base – can only be described qualitatively and subjectively (e.g. "quality improvement", which can include both "quality inspection", "process improvements", and "personnel training"). The qualitative and the subjective element in the evaluation of results obtained is also a function of the fact that, for the firm, the ultimate evaluation of the effect lies in the cost objective's ability to create revenue or reduce costs in performing other activities. This is discussed further in chapter 2.5 and 4.

9. A.J. Nanni, A, J.G. Miller & T.E. Vollmann, "What Shall We Account For? – A matrix approach relates cost data to corporate goals and strategies".
10. On closer examination, however, it proves to be the oft-met mixture of production factor cost (e.g. wages) and cost objective (e.g. machine maintenance).

**Summary**

**Characteristics of the Variability Accounting System**

1. No automatic solutions to accounting tasks.
2. The sum of production factor costs = the sum of departments' costs = the sum of costs recorded against cost objectives (including investment- as well as operation objectives).
3. It does not make use of the double-entry bookkeeping principle, but uses a pure form of statistical registration.
4. There is a hierarchy in the departmental accounts (as opposed to, for example, the job-order costing system).
5. There is a hierarchy in the objectives dimension – *plus* the fact that cost objectives other than products appear where variability factors other than the number of produced units are used. *All* costs are direct, which is achieved by establishing cost-objective accounts for the resources used or consumed by the immediate task or objective pursued.
6. Recording takes place as far down the hierarchy as a non-arbitrary allocation allows.
7. There is a distinction between direct/indirect costs in relation to objectives and *not* a general distinction between variable and fixed costs.
8. There are no depreciations in the cost accounts.
9. There are no standard costs in the accounts, but actual consumption at standard prices.
10. Only the *extra* costs of consumption/use of resources associated with additional production or activity stages is recorded against individual accounts in the objectives hierarchy. Consumption at the preceding production stage(s), is recorded against subjacent objectives (sub-objectives).
11. The detail of the account structure depends on the cost of information.
12. In answer to the question : "Which costs do we save by discontinuing production of (or activity aimed at) a given objective", the system can only automatically reply that we save what is recorded against the objective concerned plus all subjacent objectives plus eventual parts of superjacent objectives, provided that the resources can be disposed of in quantities equivalent to the cost objective. The latter is explained in chapter 1.[illegible].

## 1.1. Interpretations of and Changes in Variability Accounting Principles

The characterization of variability accounting in the previous chapter contains some interpretations and differences of content compared with Vagn Madsen's original version. In this chapter, we take a closer look at exactly what these interpretations and differences involve.

**a. The cross-reference between all three dimensions – type of production factor, department, and objective – is retained in computer-based basic records**

As opposed to the previous chapter, the original version of the variability accounting system (Vagn Madsen, 1951) did *not* keep the cross-reference between the department and objectives dimensions. The cross-reference was between production factor and department, and production factor and objectives respectively. Vagn Madsen gave the following reasons for this:

"It is certainly true that the cost statistics are so organised as to see costs and their associated variability relationships either from a department perspective or a cost-objective perspective, and we know that a good many rationalization analyses can be based not on "either/or", but must build on a combination of both. However, it would be impractical and completely unfeasible for the statistics to contain all existing combinations of departments and products, which is why we must instead insist on being able to go back to the raw data and extract the combinations which are relevant for each individual analysis."[11]

This is a reasonable and understandable explanation given the data processing technology of the time, which could boast of nothing more advanced than a punched-card system. So while the idea of maintaining – for each and every cost item – the connection between all three dimensions could probably be formulated, as the quotation shows, searches of combined criteria of production factor type, department, and cost objective would have resulted in so many sequential retrievals that any practical application would have been ruled out. With today's more powerful computers and relational database software, the cost statistics mentioned in the above quotation would simply appear through extractions carried out by the so-called report generator, with the 3-dimensional basic records being stored in the various tables of the database.

As will be seen, however, the missing cross-reference is not all that important for the analysis possibilities Vagn Madsen had in mind when he

11. Madsen, V., *Bidrag til Belysning af Rationaliseringsproblemerne i Industrivirksomheder*, p. 38.

developed the variability accounting system. This is mainly due to a different view of the concept of cost types than the one used here.

**b. Cost types are a categorization of production factors**

It is difficult to interpret exactly what is meant by cost types (Danish: omkostningsarter) within the framework of variability accounting as described by Vagn Madsen. In particular, any interpretation inevitably leads to wondering about what the fundamental difference between cost types and cost objectives is. If we start with a couple of the author's own examples – reproduced in supplement 2 – then the concept of cost types is used for a large number of costs which, in the present interpretation, appear as cost objectives. This involves all types of labour tasks. In the supplement, these are illustrated by the activities of foremen and administrative personnel in the form of "making changes and additions to specifications, plus discussions with design department", "inspection", "technical drawings", "tolerance calculations", "tests and trials", etc Of all illustrations of cost types in the figures, the only ones which are also viewed as cost types here are "materials" and its specifications. The concept of cost types used in the present work is therefore the common one, i.e. *the monetary equivalent of the factors of production*. Individual employees – blue-collar as well as white-collar workers – or groups of employees, are characterized as factors of production and their cost as production factor costs. The characterization of the tasks these employees carry out constitutes the objectives dimension. According to this view, then, production factor costs describe the monetary equivalent of *inputs* to a process, with the purpose of the process being described through its *objective*, and the monetary equivalent through its cost objective.

That Vagn Madsen does not use this conceptualization is due to the introduction of the concept of "operation" (Danish: præstation) which, from a theoretical point of view, is indistinguishable from the cost-objective concept. There were also practical considerations to take into account – considerations which can be traced back to the less advanced computer technology of the time.

The operation concept is used in the following way:[12]

"*A process is an operation with a given objective.*[13] In our statistics, we try to place operations vertically as cost types, and objectives horizontally as variability factors. If an

12. Vagn Madsen: *Bidrag til Belysning af Rationaliseringsproblemerne i Industrivirksomheder*, p. 84.
13. Quoted from R. Kristensson, *Industriel organisation*, Svensk Teknisk uppslagsbok III, p. 85, Stockholm, 1943.

operation has several adjacent objectives, then corresponding groups of variability factors are placed in the statistics." (My emphasis)

It can be remembered from the description of variability accounting in chapter 1 that every cost consumption is characterized by three dimensions: the type of production factor to be used (called production factor cost), where – in which department – the consumption has occurred, and for which immediate objective it has been used, in effect, a qualitative description of the intended result of the process.

These characteristics are confused in the above quotation. In itself, the operation concept *cannot* be used as a *new way of describing* cost consumption. Any characterization of the operation must be made on the basis of which factors of production are used in its implementation, where it takes place, or which objective it serves. The cost statistics referred to in the quotation are reproduced in supplement 2. From these, it can be seen that, as mentioned above, the description of operations as types of work – designated cost types by Vagn Madsen – occurs via a description of the objective of the operation.

Furthermore, the objectives concept is used in two different meanings in the quotation. This can be seen in the phrase "... place ... objectives horizontally ...". However, if we refer back to figure A, supplement 2, then we can see that he is actually talking about both departments and products, two different recording dimensions, of which only the one (products) – in the author's other use of the concept – is included under the designation "cost objective".

The advantage of the cost-type concept used in this book is that the production factor cost specification can be general and identical across departments, and moreover be combined with the time dimension in the acquisition and disposition of the factors of production. More about this under sections e. and f. below.[14]

Vagn Madsen's conceptualizations are undoubtedly connected with a pragmatic distinction between expedient, obligatory, continuous recording and ad hoc – possibly sample-based – recordings precipitated by the need for more detailed analyses. On the one hand, developments in data-storage and data-processing technology are moving in the direction of making continuous recording cheaper, and on the other hand, rapid changes in process technology

14. Another consequence of the present interpretation of the operation concept – as a cost objective description – is that Vagn Madsen's sentence "If an operation has several objectives...." does not make sense here. An "operation" cannot serve several objectives. The fact that an activity serves several objectives results in its cost record being "pushed up the hierarchy", thereby – in Vagn Madsen's words – becoming direct in relation to this higher-level objective.

and product lines are decreasing the value of the data. This results in a choice which is both pragmatical and economical by nature, and which cannot be determined theoretically. In practice, the line is drawn by laying down a minimum obligatory entry level in the chart of accounts – most often dictated by the information needs of the central accounting department – and letting further specification be left open to decentralized users. In company practice, the obligatory specification in the objectives dimension – typically differentiated per production factor and per department – is designated "objective", while additional specification is called "task". This ensures a workable distinction between a registration *requirement* and a technologically feasible registration *ability*. Here, however, we do not distinguish between registration objectives and registration tasks.

**c. Variability factors are assigned to cost objectives only**

In Vagn Madsen's variability accounting system, both department and cost objectives appear as variability factors, as the following quotation clearly shows:

"We seek therefore to record cost types for both individual cost centres, with whose size, organisation, and degree of employment they vary, and cost objectives, with whose qualitative and quantitative size they likewise vary. One can always change the costs by either changing the cost centres or the cost objectives, or both simultaneously. Accordingly, costs vary with both individual departments, sub-departments, or groups thereof, and with the cost objectives, and the problem is to make these variation relationships as visible as possible in the records. Since a knowledge of these relationships is a necessary condition for rationalization analyses, and since we want to systematize the recording according to this principle, designated the variability principle, we call both the individual cost centres and the cost objectives variability factors."[15]

This is a somewhat unfortunate turn of phrase, seeing that, in the same breath, the variability principle is formulated in the following way:

"By variability principle, we mean that costs are placed as closely as possible to the factors with whose quantitative changes they vary, on the reasoning that one can only influence costs by changing these quantitative factors, provided factor prices are constant."[16]

In the interpretation of variability accounting presented in the previous chapter, the idea of the *department as variability factor is abandoned*. The reason for this is that it is not considered possible to change a department's costs without also changing its activities, which must either be effected through (i) a change

15. Madsen, op. cit., pp. 22-23.
16. Madsen, op. cit. p. 21.

in the activities which are assigned to the department (more or fewer objectives), (ii) more/fewer performances of the same activities, or (iii) a change in quality. According to this view, then, costs *always* have a qualitative or quantitative effect on the objectives, which is why variability factors are only assigned to these. This is not to trivialize the importance of the department dimension in analysing and explaining cost development, only to abandon the designation "variability factor" for it, since it is not logically possible to say "factors with whose quantitative changes costs vary" without these factors being variability factors of the objectives at the same time. In this connection, it is worth noting that it is precisely the retained cross-reference between the department and objectives dimensions which ensures the preservation of the individual department's influence on an interdepartmental cost objective.

**d. A variability factor is a measure of output – a load factor unit**

What, then, is a variability factor? The most pressing question is whether this quantitative factor is a common measure of an activity's (an objective's) input factors – i.e. a measure of the production factors used and/or consumed in carrying out an activity – or it is an output factor – i.e. a quantitative measure of the activity's output. Vagn Madsen does not discuss the concept in any more detail than in the quotation above (cf. this and the previous chapter), but he does give a number of examples, including, amongst others, the number of products, number of product parts, and the number of production batches.

On this basis, the variability factor must be interpreted as a measure of output. At the same time, however, it is also stated that "the costs should vary approximately proportionately with this", so there are reasons for questioning this interpretation.

A more realistic assumption would be that the *consumption and use of production factor services* varies approximately proportionately with the variability factor (interpreted as an output measure). This is the same as assuming that for each activity/objective there is an approximately linear production function in production factor services. On the other hand, costs depend on the quantum nature of the production factors – more about this in section e. below. If we assume that there is an approximate proportionality between the factors of production and costs, then it is the same as saying that we have an approximately constant price function, or that the price is approximately independent of the acquired quantity.

So if we stick to the interpretation of a variability factor as a measure of output – as in the previous chapter – then this measure must be expressed in a form which allows the production factors' output capacity to be expressed in the same way. For factors of production which are only involved in the production of a single objective (activity), there are many possibilities. In all other cases, which is the most common in a well-developed objectives chart of accounts, these variability factors must all be converted to a common measure – the measures must be homogenized, so to speak – which at the same time can also be used to express the volume of capacity. A typical measure would be "hours" – employee hours, machine hours, etc. A good measure for these two types of production factors is Böhm and Wille's concept of Standard-Belegungsstunden, SBS (standard capacity hours), in which planned and actual output can be expressed at the same time as available capacity can be expressed both in this and in orthodox hours.[17]

### e. The meaning of "direct" and "indirect" costs in the department and objectives dimensions

Since there is no universally-accepted definition of direct and indirect costs, the sense in which these concepts are used in variability accounting must be made clear. Figure 3 below presents four possible interpretations.

**Figure 3:** Possible interpretations of direct and indirect costs in the department- and objectives dimensions.

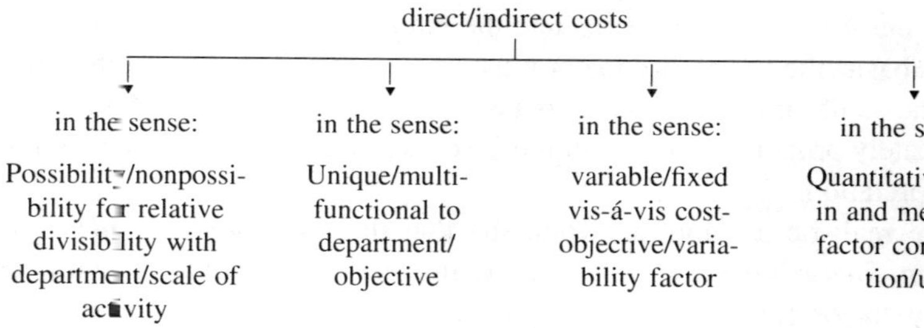


The interpretation of direct and indirect costs depends on whether we look at them from the department dimension or the objectives dimension:

#### *e.1. The objectives dimension*

The first criterion to be established in this dimension results from *relativizing the concepts fixed and variable production factor consumption.* By this is meant that we see which resource consumption varies or does not vary (i.e. is

17. H.H. Böhm & F. Wille: *Deckungsbeitragsrechnung und Optimierung*, p. 132ff.

fixed) with an increase or a decrease in a given variability factor. This can be illustrated by the costs of book-publishing. The costs of the printing plate are fixed in relation to the number of books printed. Accordingly, the costs of the printing plate are assignable not to the number of copies of the book but only to the book title. The number of pages in the copies can serve as a variability factor for printing plate costs, and the number of books as a variability factor for paper, ink, and binding costs. Note that in the relativized use of the concepts fixed and variable, there is no mention of the time-horizon in acquisition and discharge of resources. In other words, it is *not* possible to couple the oft-met phrase "all costs are variable in the long run" with a relative use of fixed and variable, because what is actually meant by this phrase is that "all costs are reversible in the long run". Therefore, the first criterion for assigning costs to a given objective in a variability accounting system is that the consumption or use of the production factor in question varies (approximately proportionately) with increases and decreases in the variability factor. Those costs which, in the relativized use of fixed and variable, are characterized as variable, can, in principle, display both over- and under-proportionality, as a function of both non-linear activity functions and price functions.

The second criterion is that the physical factor consumption/use (measured in physical quantities consumed or time used) actually *is measured* as a consumed input of the objective in question. If not – it can have been dropped due to the high cost of registration – then the monetary equivalent of this consumption must be recorded against a higher-level objective (in which all the objectives which use this resource are found as sub-objectives) in the cost statistics of the variability accounting system.

The two other criteria deal with the extent to which the factor of production has unique or multifunctional possibilities in the objectives dimension, and with its absolute and relative divisibility with the scale of activity, as measured by the variability factor. If a factor of production is *unique* to an objective, there is no problem in attributing its cost to this objective – irrespective of its absolute or relative divisibility.[18] If it is *multifunctional*, on the other hand, which is the most likely in an elaborate objectives structure, then it will depend on the absolute and relative divisibility of the production factor. But it will also depend on the desired level of reliability or objectivity in the

18. This applies if the system has to support decisions such as whether a particular objective should be maintained in its entirety or dropped altogether. If the system also has to support incremental decisions, then a supplement, in the form of information on the factor's absolute divisibility, is needed, together with information on the time necessary to remove or discharge the production factor. See, in addition, section [illegible].

economic description. The consequence of a very high (up to 100%) preferred level of reliability is that a production factor which is not completely relatively divisible with the variability factor cannot be assigned to the objective concerned, but must instead be recorded against an objective at a level which contains the objectives which use that particular resource as sub-objectives. Such a rigorous criterion would mean that even those materials which could only be purchased in a minimum quantity greater than that needed for the objective, would have to be "pushed up the hierarchy". This would even apply to hourly-paid labour. Put another way, we are here talking about applying a very strict principle of non-arbitrariness. Employing a criterion of up-to-100% reliability – relating to the absolute and relative divisibility of the resource – also has the consequence that the concept of costs becomes identical with the concept acquisition cost.[19] There is no problem in applying such a rigorous criterion, but it will have the consequence of greatly diluting the potency of the cost accounts, because most of the information on cost will be transferred to data-manipulation outside the accounts, using the physical recordings in the factor input statistics and the cost of acquisition in the financial accounts as a basis.

Here – as with Vagn Madsen – the criterion on which the attributability of costs to a specific objective in the objectives hierarchy is based, is that the physical consumption is measured as that used on the objective *and* that the consumption/use of the production factor varies approximately proportionately with the objective's variability factor. The criteria for the absolute and relative divisibility of the production factor are not used in this cost dimension.[20]

One consequence of this choice is that the cost evaluation of the factor consumption is divorced from the actual purchase price of the factors of production. However, the principle involved in the transition from quantity and time recording to cost evaluation is the "Pagatoric principle", according to which imputed costs, in the form of opportunity costs, depreciations, and imputed interest, are not counted as cost categories in the variability accounting system.[21]

### *e.2. The department dimension*

If we now turn our attention to a definition of direct and indirect costs in rela-

19. This applies to the conceptual content, but not necessarily to the time parameter.
20. This is in contrast to the criteria on which Paul Riebel bases his "Grundrechnung" - cf. P. Riebel *Einzelkosten- und Deckungsbeitragsrechnung*.
21. There is agreement with Paul Riebel on this point, cf. op. cit. See, in addition, Poul E. Sørensen "Indledende betragtninger over behovet for et ændret omkostningsregistreringsbegreb".

tion to the department dimension, the first thing to note is that the relativized use of fixed and variable costs is unimportant. This results solely from the fact that we have dropped the department dimension as a variability factor.

Before proceeding, however, we must be clear about what type of department concept is used. Do we mean a budgetary responsibility-derived concept, an organisational/implementational-derived concept, or a physical/geographical location? The differences can be illustrated by a manufacturing trial run of a product prototype in the production department. The trial will typically be the budgetary responsibility of the product development manager, though the organisational responsibility will remain with the production manager. The physical location is the machine where the test run takes place. It is this physical location which constitutes the lowest level in variability accounting's department hierarchy. The overlying hierarchies follow the organisational/implementational hierarchy. The budgetary responsibility-derived concept of department is not used. This is not to overlook the usefulness of delegating budgetary responsibility, just that, to the extent that it is not implicit in the other dimensions, it must be established as an additional recording dimension. It will be clear in the example that the objective is "product development" (possibly specified by a particular prototype), thus pointing to the product development manager's budget. In addition to this, however, it will also be apparent from the simultaneously recorded location that the actual responsibility for this task is shared with the production department.

The criterion used for direct attributability of costs in the department dimension is "quantitatively put in and measured factor consumption/use". The divisibility and nature of the production factor – whether multifunctional or unique – have no bearing on this, and are not used. A cost is thus assigned as far down the department hierarchy as the quantitative – non-monetary – recordings allow. As far as interdepartmental services are concerned (e.g. maintenance), the department dimension reflects the "supplying department". If the receiving department, or location, is important for evaluating the variability, then it must be reflected in the contemporaneous objectives dimension through additional descriptive attributes (e.g. maintenance specified by machine or machine class). In the department dimension, considerations concerning cost of information can also lead to decisions not to measure factor consumption in as much detail as possible, leaving the equivalent cost to be assigned to higher-level departments.

### f. The handling of unique and multifunctional costs, the divisibility of the factors of production, and reversibility

Section e. showed that the uniqueness/multifunctionality and divisibility of the factors of production did not determine the attributability of costs in the department or objectives dimensions. This does not mean that they cannot be dealt with in a recording system, however. Thus the unique/multifunctional nature of the factors of production is contained de facto in this interpretation of variability accounting, even though the criterion is not used for the assignment of costs in any particular dimension.

Because the cross-reference between production factor cost, department cost and cost objective is preserved, a variability accounting record will show whether a production factor is multifunctional or unique. Here, a production factor is namely multifunctional – as regards the department as well as the objectives dimensions – if it appears from the simultaneous department and objectives dimensions that the cost equivalent shows up in two or more department- or two or more objectives accounts respectively. Finally, the total accounts code – showing all three dimensions – will reveal whether the production factor in question is complexly multifunctional, meaning that it appears in both several departments and several objectives. Both types of searches can be carried out without a hitch in relational databases. The qualities in question are especially interesting if the production factor's price is a function of the quantity acquired, or if a production factor's efficient utilization depends on total use, and not just on its use towards a specific objective. It must be left to calculations *outside* the accounts to evaluate the economic importance of these two circumstances, however.

*The handling of absolute divisibility demands additional registrations.* The absolute divisibility of the factors of production is connected with their quantum nature, which refers to a minimum purchase quantity as far as consumable factors are concerned (e.g. materials), and the number of units of capacity as far as capacity resources are concerned (including tangible assets of any kind and numbers of employees within each profession, including subcategories of blue-collar workers). Absolute divisibility is unimportant as far as the latter group is concerned if the specification of costs is so detailed that each unit of capacity (individual people and machines) appear as separate production factors. The advantage of using such a detailed specification of costs is that, compared with a more aggregated recording, there is no loss of information. On the other hand, since the information will primarily be useful in the firm's planning process, there is a good case for classifying according to homogeneity in qualitative service potential – i.e. types of equipment and machinery, and categories of employees – and, in addition, the number of capacity units making up the total capacity within each group (cf. figure 4 below). In the case of consumable input factors, minimum acquisition/purchase quantities are recorded for the relevant factors.

A natural continuation of this is yet *another dimension* of the production factor, namely its *disposition time* (i.e. the time horizon for acquisition and discharge of a resource/production factor). By using such a recording dimension, concrete information can be obtained about the earliest date of reversibility (see figure 4). For personnel and leased equipment, the relevant information is contractual terms of notice, for certain consumable factors (e.g. materials supplied on annual contracts), it is renegotiation dates, whereas for owned plant and machinery, it is either not specified or it is stated as the remaining expected service life of the asset. This treatment of absolute divisibility and reversibility goes beyond the capability of variability accounting. With the interpretations and changes made in this and the previous chapter, however, such an extension becomes more obvious and even straightforward.

Based on the variability recordings, relative divisibility – i.e. production-factor divisibility relative to activities/objectives – can be *evaluated but not determined*. This evaluation can be carried out in relation to (i) a single run (an individual performance) of an objective – in relation to which no production factor is likely to be completely relatively divisible, however, (ii) the total performance of an objective over an accounting period, or (iii) in those cases where a factor is multifunctional, by converting the specific unit of measurement per variability factor – called load factor units[22] – to a common capacity utilization measure, in which the capacity of the production factor can also be measured (e.g. via Böhm and Wille's previously-mentioned "Standard Belegungsstunden").

The concepts used in this chapter to clarify the interpretation of the variability accounting system are grouped together in figure 4 below.

### g. The relationship between cost-objectives and variability factors

Vagn Madsen, as the quotations show, operates with a close connection between the concepts "objective" and "variability factors". Objectives are literally defined by the fact that there is a common factor with which costs vary approximately proportionately.[23] Such a close connection is not

22. This was originally coined by Zakken Worre: *Noter til internt regnskabsvæsen*, and developed further in his *Registrering og styring af kapacitetsomkostninger*. For a discussion of the connection between variability factors and load factor units (Danish: belastningsenheder), see Israelsen: "Lader Vagn Madsens og Zaken Worres tanker og ideer om virksomhedens omkostningsregnskab sig forene?"

    Worre only uses the concept in connection with capacity costs, whereas here it is used in a general sense, since, in a recording context, there is no distinction between variable- and capacity costs.

23. Cf. quotation in chapter 1.

**Figure 4**: Dimensions of factors of production and their use as a basis for the elaboration of a cost accounting system.

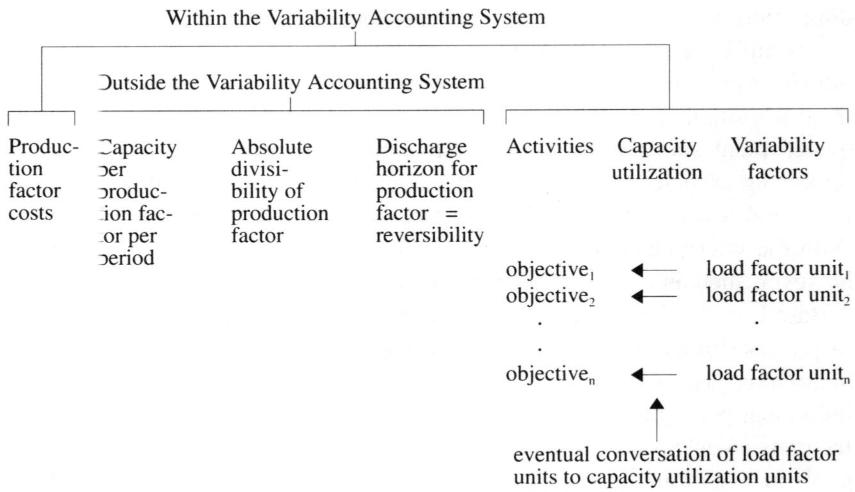


employed here. In this interpretation, objectives are defined on the basis of activities which can be isolated and controlled relatively autonomously, and for which it is therefore possible to frame policies for their quantitative and qualitative implementation. The variability factor (or more precisely, the specific load factor unit measure chosen) helps explain and forecast the development in actual and budgeted costs of the objective concerned.

The difficulty of maintaining a close connection between the objective and the variability factors is especially apparent in the higher-level objectives, something which Vagn Madsen also acknowledges:

> "We have now moved so far away from subjacent concepts and towards superjacent concepts (in the objectives dimension) that it is no longer possible to indicate an unambiguous variability factor. The relevant factors must depend on the purpose of the calculation."[24] (My brackets)

At the higher-level objectives are costs – resulting from the above-mentioned recording principles – which, on the basis of the criterion "relativized variable/fixed", vary with the range of activity under the objective concerned. But there are also costs which have been assigned here because considerations of information cost have ruled out a recording of input quantities which would

24. Madsen, *Regnskabsvæsenets opgaver og problemer – i ny belysning*, p. 141.

have enabled a lower-level assignment. Typically, these two types of costs will not be expected to vary with the same variability factor. In this situation the preserved cross-reference between the three dimensions comes in useful, because now we can look for a variability factor which can, with reasonable accuracy, explain and/or forecast costs for the combined production factor type/department/objective case.

**h. The practical structure of the recordings in the objectives dimension**
According to the previous delineation, description in the objectives dimension encompasses a number of recordings, e.g. "type of work", "receiving department of internal services", etc.. This could give the impression that the chart of accounts – the practical tool for codifying the various types of activities – will become extremely detailed. This can be avoided if tools such as relational database software are used. The computerized organisation of the objectives dimension will therefore consist in a systematization of each of its attributes: a codification of "types of work", of "(receiving) departments", "products", "product parts", etc., letting each of these attributes constitute a separate column in a table of the objectives dimension. There are also examples in practice of chart of accounts – inspired by variability accounting – segmented into innumerable attributes. The present theoretical determination of the content of the objectives dimension must therefore not be confused with the "attributes" of computer terminology. It is just that, as already mentioned, one often has to use several attributes in characterizing costs in the objectives dimension.

**Summary**
The changes and clarifications which have been made to Vagn Madsen's variability accounting system are summarized in the following points, which can thus also be regarded as an elaboration of the fundamental features of the system as outlined in chapter 1.

a. The cross-reference between variability accounting's three recording dimensions is kept in computer-based basic recordings, which means that different combinations of information can be retrieved as desired both between the dimensions and in larger or smaller sub-groups of them.
b. Production factor costs are a categorization of the factors of production acquired from outside the firm. Production factors which the firm manufactures itself as part of its value-adding process – e.g. in-house components – appear in the firm's production statistics under both input and output. As output, it is the actual volume produced which is recorded

against the component objective concerned, while as input the in-house component is recorded as a "type of production factor" consumed in connection with the use of the component in the value-adding process. In variability accounting's *cost* statistics, however, in-house components are recorded only as output, i.e. as cost objectives.

c. Variability factors are only assigned to the cost objectives – not to the department dimension – since it is not considered possible to change a department's costs without at the same time changing its activities.
d. A variability factor is a measure for the output of a given objective. The concrete measure used here is designated the "load factor unit".
e. Only the direct costs of a given objective are recorded against that objective's account. The same applies to a given department. In the objectives dimension, "direct" means that the quantitative – non-monetary – resource input must be (directly) measured as that consumed/utilized, and that the resource input must be expected to vary approximately proportionately with an increase or decrease in the variability factor. In the department dimension – which is the supplying department – the only requirement is that the factor consumption is (directly) measured.
f. Whether a production factor cost is unique or multifunctional – which is of interest when the price and/or efficiency of the production factor depends on its overall use – can be determined by means of variability accounting's three-dimensional sets of recordings. A factor of production is therefore unique to a department or an objective as long as it only appears in one department or one objectives account, otherwise it is multifunctional.

   A recording basis for the evaluation of the absolute divisibility and reversibility of a production factor and its equivalent costs demands recordings over and above – though in simple continuation of – those of the variability accounting system (cf. figure 4).
g. There is no requirement for a one-to-one relation between objectives and variability factors. Objectives are defined on the principle that it must be possible to draw up relatively autonomous policies for the area of activity concerned. There is no need for a one-to-one relation when the cross-reference between the three recording dimensions is kept, since one can try to identify variability factors for the combination production factor/objective or – more detailed – production factor/department/objective.
h. The objectives dimension can be usefully described in the database tables using more adjacent attributes. On the other hand, it should be remembered that there is a recording hierarchy between the objectives, but not between the attributes.

# 2. Fundamental Features of the Original Activity-Based Costing System

The primary aim of the original ABC system – called simply ABC in this chapter, another designation being suggested for the new orientation of the system in chapter 3 – was to attain a better calculation of product costs. "Better" here compared with the product costs of traditional full-cost-based cost systems, which allocate indirect product costs[25] among the manufactured products using one, or just a few, allocation bases based on production volume (product-direct labour/wages, machine hours, direct materials, etc.). The unwise decisions which have been made in pricing and product policies, marketing, design, and choice of process, etc., as a result of letting production costs calculated in this way act as a basis for decision-making have recently been documented in several articles by Cooper and Kaplan (see bibliography).[26] Thanks to, among others, Vagn Madsen's work, Scandinavians are already well-versed in many of the shortcomings of traditional cost systems.

The way to avoid making wrong decisions is by constructing a form of cost accounts which only uses volume-dependent allocation bases for those categories of indirect product costs which vary with them, and by introducing other *volume-unrelated* activity measures – designated "Cost Drivers" – for other groups of costs. It is especially the latter which make comparisons with variability accounting both natural and rewarding.

25. Depending on the specific layout of the traditional cost accounts, the indirect product costs allocated among the products include not only production costs but also purchasing- and sales department costs.
26. These authors' documentation also includes variable costing. For an evaluation of the quality of documentation under both systems, see Israelsen and Sørensen, "Nye Økonomistyringsudfordringer".

## 2.1. Activity-Based Costing Compared with Variability Accounting

The most important ingredients in an ABC system can be described by referring to Robin Cooper's figure (figure 5) below:

**Figure 5**: Activity-based Cost Systems as a Two Stage Allocation Procedure.

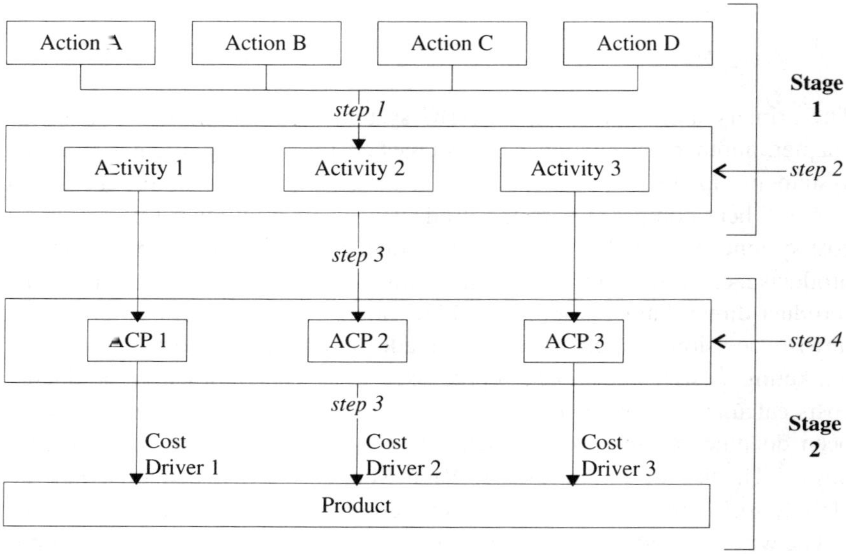


Source: Robin Cooper, "The Rise of Activity-based Costing – Part Four: What do Activity-based Cost Systems Look Like?", *Journal of Cost Management,* Spring, 1989, p. 39 (with the addition of Cooper's steps). Reprinted by permission of Warran, Gorham & Lamont; all rights reserved.

According to Robin Cooper, five main design choices are involved in working out an ABC system. These are shown in figure 5 as steps 1-5, and are examined in more detail below in a comparison with the corresponding design choices of the variability accounting system. By this means, the similarities and differences of the two systems can be identified. Some of the weaknesses of the ABC system are pointed out and illustrated in chapters 2.2 – 2.5, while the analysis also enables further clarification of the qualities of the variability accounting system.

The five design choices of the ABC system – with accompanying short descriptions – are:

Step 1: Aggregating actions into activities
Since no feasible accounting system can hope to describe the performance of every single action, they must be grouped into "activities". A product's consumption of an activity – not its consumption of "actions" – forms the basis of the system's calculation of product costs, the accuracy of which is thus affected by the choice of aggregation level.

Step 2: Reporting the cost of activities
Here, it is decided which actions within each activity to report costs for. The choice has no bearing on the accuracy of product costs, cf. step 1, only on the reporting depth.

Step 3: Selecting the first-stage allocation bases
This aims at establishing the method by which the total costs of carrying out an activity are determined. The method involves both "direct measurement" and "indirect estimation". The method results in an "Activity Cost Pool" (ACP) per activity.

Step 4: Identifying the activity centres
Several organisational segments can be involved in carrying out an activity, and thus in consuming the costs in the associated ACP. In this design phase, it is decided whether to report in an aggregated form, or separately for each organisational segment, called "Activity Centre". Again, the choice does not affect the accuracy of product costs.

Step 5: Selecting second-stage Cost Drivers
A product's costs are estimated in relation to its consumption of the respective activities. This design step consists in finding a measure of activity (Cost Driver) for each activity which reflects the resource consumption of that activity, and which can thus form the basis for a calculation of costs per unit of the Cost Driver (ACP divided by the total number of Cost-Driver units). The product's costs are subsequently presented as a summation of costs for the number of Cost-Driver units of the respective activities it has used.

*Step 1: Aggregating actions into activities*

Recording every single action in the firm is regarded as being prohibitively expensive. So if the firm wants a feasible and economically justifiable system, the individual actions must be aggregated. Not just a grouping of qualitatively identical single action (e.g. transporting a specific quantity of a given raw material from the warehouse to a particular production site) into actions (all materials-transport actions of the stated type, or more broadly grouped into all actions of internal transport of materials together), but a grouping of such homogeneous actions into a complex of actions called an "activity". Cooper gives the example that all actions connected with setup can be treated as the activity "setup", which embraces such actions as:

"...new tools have to be drawn from the tool room, inserted, and qualified. The feeds and speeds of the machine must be altered, parts moved from inventory storage to the shop floor, the first part has to be inspected, the batch scheduled, and so on".[27]

However, it is in the nature of things that the greater the number of actions aggregated to one activity – i.e. the greater the number of homogeneous services incorporated in a complex service – the less it is likely that the relative quantity ratio between the included homogeneous actions can be preserved unchanged with the performances of that activity. This has at least two consequences:

(1) If a product's manufacturing precept shows that it involves the use of a particular activity, while in fact it conceals variations in the use of subsets of the included homogeneous actions, then, on account of information cost, it will lead to inaccuracies in the description of the costs of that product. This is not only true of the actual physical production, but also of a number of supporting activities, e.g. purchasing, production planning, and selling.
(2) It is difficult to identify production bottlenecks because apparent surplus capacity – in relation to the accuracy of description used – might actually be scarce, on account of local bottlenecks within the activity concerned.

Similar aggregations take place in the variability accounting system. This can be seen from the quotation in chapter 1 concerning variability factors, where aggregation was necessary precisely because of considerations of information costs.

*Step 2: Reporting the cost of activities*
For Cooper this is a question of the detail of production-cost-, and subsequently product-cost-, reporting, not of the accuracy or precision in the calculation of product costs. Cooper gives the example that setup costs can be reported either as one aggregated amount ($6) or as two (or more), e.g.

27. Op. cit, pp. 38-39.

"machine setup" ($4) and "material movement" ($2). The relationship between "actions" and "activities" is shown in figure 6.

**Figure 6**: Illustration of the relationship between "activities" and "actions".

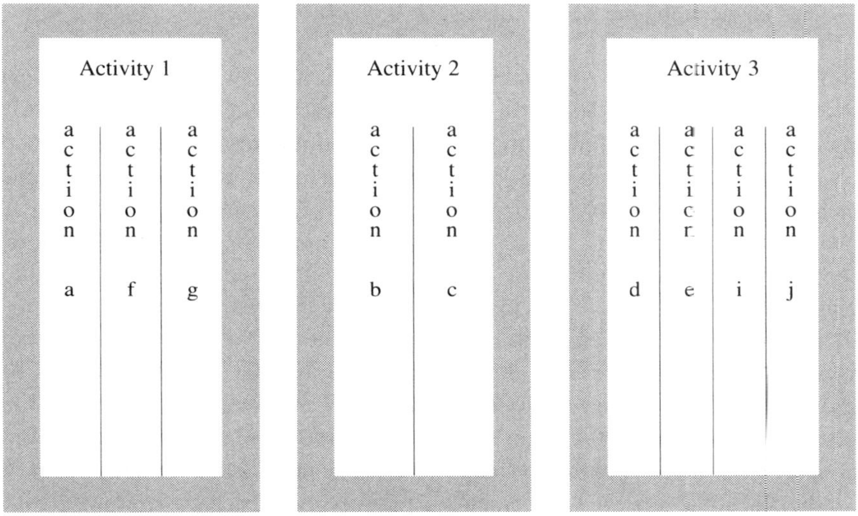


If we want the possibility, in the ABC system, of reporting the costs of carrying out actions, then we have to *measure* and record their resource consumption. In other words, the cost consumption of the respective actions does *not* result from a pro rata allocation (allocation base) of the total costs of an activity.

This information need can be met in two ways in the variability accounting system:

(1) If aggregated reporting is desired, then one objective only, with the designation "setup", is established in the objectives dimension. As a rule, however, simultaneous recording in the department dimension will show that more than one department has been involved in the activity – illustrated in the example by the departments responsible for "machine setup" and "in-house transportation". In this case, therefore, disaggregated reporting is possible if desired, even with the use of the aggregated objectives dimension. However, it should be pointed out that this is not necessary, since the choice of reporting mode in the variability accounting system is distinct from the recording task.

(2) In cases where the same department is responsible for both machine setup and materials movement, and the possibility for disaggregated reporting is desired, then two adjacent objectives are established in the objectives dimension, called "machine setup" and "materials movement". In Cooper's example, one would, in variability accounting terminology, be using the same variability factor for both objectives.

Neither of the above two solutions would mean a wider range of recording than that required by Cooper's. However, the advantage of the variability accounting solution is that, using the established recording scope, one is not obliged to continue using the same variability factor, but can at any time change it to suit the recording depth of costs. This is carried out in solution (2) above by using separate factors per objective, and in solution (1) by using separate factors per combination of department/objective. However, introducing additional variability factors results in an expansion of the recording scope in order to measure and register the number of units of the new variability factor (load factor units) concerned. In Cooper's example this is shown by the recording of "number of setups" as the variability factor for resources consumed in the setup activity, excluding those consumed in material movements, *and* "number of material movements" as the variability factor for the objective "material movements" or the combined department/objectives dimension "in-house transportation/setups". On the other hand, no further recording of resource consumption is required. In both the ABC and variability accounting systems, cost consumption is disaggregated in the complex set of actions, "setup", and the action "material movement".

Even in the case where the same department carries out several of the actions we want to report, we *might* be able to capture this via the production factor dimension in the variability accounting system without having to establish several "objectives". If, for example, employees working on the two types of actions were paid differently, then it could be reported via this identification of the resource consumption.

*Step 3: Selecting the first-stage allocation bases*

This design choice presents us with a choice which determines the accuracy of the recording, and with it the evaluation of costs per activity.

As Cooper's figure (reproduced here as figure 5) shows, there is a one-on-one relationship between the choice of activity and choice of Activity Cost Pool (ACP), in the sense that all the costs of carrying out a given activity are placed in one and the same ACP, and each performance of a particular activity is – with a starting point in the accompanying ACP – costed equally.

Henceforth, the greater the desired recording accuracy of actual cost consumption, the greater the number of activities and ACPs the cost-recording system has to accommodate.

Cooper's own example of the resources consumed in the setup of two different machine classes is illuminating:

*If* the resources consumed in various setups are different, and *if*, on account of recording cost, one chooses to ignore this, then the calculation of actual resource consumption per type of setup will naturally be less accurate (unless the more detailed recording volume in itself leads to a greater proportion of recording errors). However, the bias of the introduced error – in the sense of which type of setup is over- and undercosted – depends on the simultaneous choice of allocation base, as the following quotation from Cooper shows:

"For example, if setup costs are traced to the two types of machines using the allocation base "number of setup hours", then the cost system assumes that each machine class consumes the same quantity of resources per setup hour. For the machine class that consumes more resources per setup hour, reported setup costs will be too low. In contrast, the allocation base "number of setups" assumes that all setups consume the same quantity of resources irrespective of duration and machine class. In this system, the machine class that takes longer to set up will be undercosted. Thus, the level and nature of the distortion introduced depends on the allocation base used for indirect estimation in the first stage".[28]

What does this design choice look like in the variability accounting system?

Provided the most detailed recording is not considered prohibitively expensive, the following solution is chosen: two setup cost objectives – e.g. called "setup – machine class I" and "setup – machine class II" – are established. This is exactly analogous to Cooper having to choose two activities and their two corresponding ACPs *and, by direct measurement, record* the cost consumption of the two activities. No distortion in cost information is introduced through this solution (though in practice one might end up with a potentially greater number of measuring and recording errors).

The possibility of identifying the resource consumption of the two types of setup via the department dimension – similar to that outlined in design step 2 – is not feasible here. Normally, it is not the supplying department (the department responsible for the setup activities) which varies from task to task, but the receiving department, or machine class. Such a solution would necessitate expanding the variability accounting system to include not only the supplying department, but also the receiving department/machine class. As

28. Op. cit., p. 40.

indicated above and discussed in chapter 1.1, however, this takes place more appropriately via the objectives dimension.

If aggregated recording is preferred, then there is just one setup cost objective in the objectives dimension, with exactly the same consequences of inaccuracy in estimating the setup costs of the two machine classes as under the ABC system. Here, however, we come to a ***significant difference*** between the ABC system and variability accounting: with aggregated recording, neither an allocation of setup costs to the two setup categories, nor a calculation of the setup costs per setup which are subsequently allocated to a given production batch or product unit, is carried out *in* the variability accounting system – whether differentiated per machine class or aggregated. This would take place *outside* the variability accounting system, with this system as the source of information. Variability accounting is, after all, a multifunctional basic accounting system, used for solving a great many other tasks than just the ex post calculation of product unit costs. Conversely, within the ABC system, and without breaking its inherent principles, one can operate with Activity Cost Pools which are "estimated indirectly" – cf. the above quotation. Taking Cooper's example, in an ABC system we would therefore be able to use two ACPs for setup costs – one for "setup – machine class I" and one for "setup – machine class II" – *without directly measuring* the costs consumed, but solely on the basis of an allocation base (e.g. "number of setups") which allocates the total setup costs which are measured directly in relation to the aggregated setup (see figure 7).

**Figure 7**: Establishing an Activity Cost Pool in the ABC system using allocation bases – no equivalent in the variability accounting system.

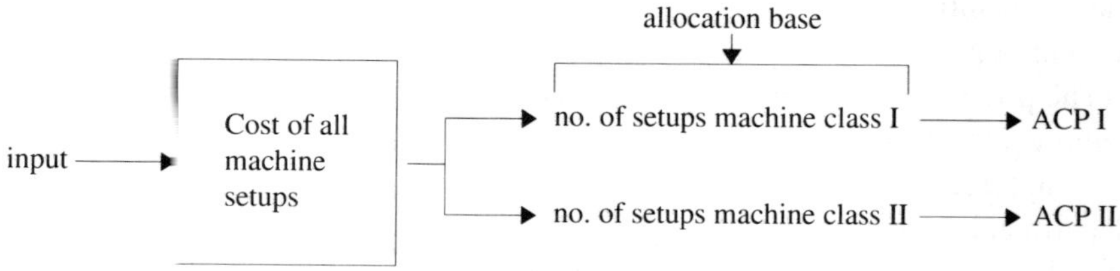


If we do not use *measurements* of resource consumption as the basis for the formation of ACPs, then we cannot, on the basis of accounting records and measurements of the number of utilized units of first-stage allocation bases, establish or verify (i.e. calculate ex post) a differentiated consumption of resources connected with setup of the two machine classes, either.

However, not verifying the resource consumption per machine class does not mean that we cannot still hypothesize that it is different, and allow this supposition to influence the choice of allocation base. Basing the creation of ACPs on allocations, rather than on measurements, means choosing the allocation base which best reflects the actual resource consumption of carrying out the respective activities. In other words, an allocation which comes as close as possible to that which could have been obtained by direct measurement. Cooper has taken this into consideration, though with the limitation that the allocation base selected must allocate an *equal* amount per unit of the base. This seems unnecessary, and can be illustrated by reference to Cooper's setup example:

If we presume that the setup of one machine class consumes more resources than the setup of another, and, furthermore, that the resource consumption is a function of the product for which setup is being undertaken, then we can consider letting *standard* costs per setup be the allocation base for *actual* costs. So if we have carried out an aggregated recording of the costs of the activity setup, plus recorded "number of setups" per product per machine class, over several accounting periods – with a presumed different amount of setup activity for each machine class – then the proposed differentiated cost rate per setup can perhaps prove to provide a more reliable description of the variation in total actual setup costs than an undifferentiated rate. In which case, the differentiated rate is much to be preferred. Appendix B contains a numerical example of this.

Cooper gives the impression – though not expressed explicitly - that the design choices in steps 1 and 3 are sequential, while in actual fact, since the reliability of the data embodied in the accounting system has to be taken into account, they must be simultaneous. The level chosen for aggregating homogeneous actions into activities (complex actions) under step 1 also determines the costs of inputs which have to be recorded in the equivalent ACP. If a first-stage allocation base (design step 3) which, with the desired level of accuracy, reflects the actual resource consumption of each performance of an activity cannot be found at this level of aggregation, then there is nothing for it but to go back to design step 1 and disaggregate the chosen activity.[29] In principle, disaggregation can take place in two different ways, which, in terms of Cooper's example, can be formulated as follows: (i) New actions, e.g. "direct setup hours – machine class I" and "direct setup hours –

29. This problem occurs both when the activity embraces heterogeneous – i.e. qualitatively different – actions from performance to performance, and when the resource consumption of included actions are a function of the task at hand.

machine class II", can be introduced, while all other actions are kept in one group, comprising "setup excluding direct setup hours", which is undifferentiated as regards machine classes; (ii) Alternatively, one can establish two ACPs which, for all involved actions, are differentiated according to machine class.

*Step 4: Identifying the activity centres*
What this entails can be illustrated by making a slight addition to figure 6 (see fig. 8 below).

**Figure 8**: Illustration of the Activity Centre concept.

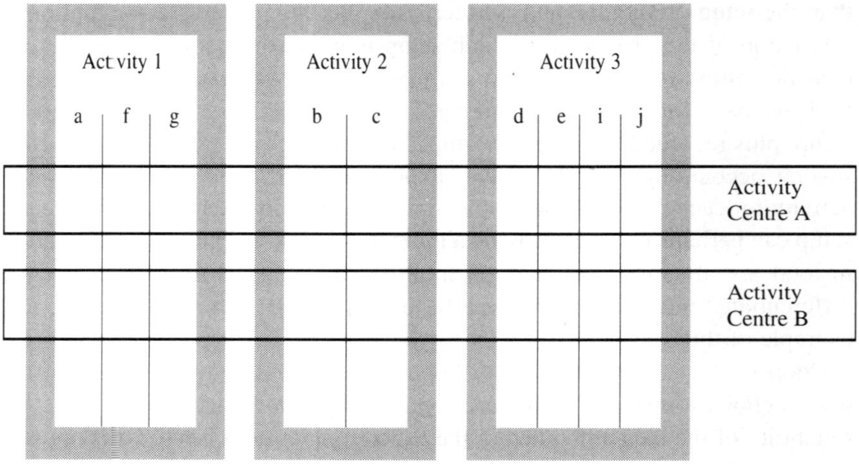


Note: a, f, g etc., represent "actions".

The choice of *Activity Centre* is important to the detail which the cost accounts can report on the organisational location of elements of an activity, but not for the accuracy of the costs per activity. Cooper gives the example that the ABC system can report product costs either as $50 or as $30 for manufacturing and $20 for receiving.

This design choice thus corresponds to variability accounting's choice of specification in the department dimension. It must again be emphasized, however, that these costs are not allocated per product, or per product unit, in the variability accounting system. There is the very **significant difference**, however, that, as opposed to variability accounting's department dimension, there is *no hierarchical structure in the ABC system's activity centres*, which means that they have no "superjacent centres". Put another way, the organisational hierarchy is "compressed" in the ABC system, since all the costs which figure in the estimation of product costs must appear in one or more of a number of adjacent activity centres. This is a feature which the system has in common with traditional job-order and process-costing systems, but its applicability is not as problematic in the ABC system, precisely because it operates – as opposed to the traditional systems – with many other activities than direct production activities. Or, using ABC terminology, many other drivers than volume-related ones.

*Step 5: Selecting second-stage Cost Drivers*
This design phase is about finding a Cost Driver for every activity which, on the one hand reflects resource consumption, and with it costs (estimated in the accompanying ACP), and on the other hand can be used as a basis for reflecting the various product's utilization of these activities. In turn, the product's utilization of the various activities forms the basis of the ABC's calculations of the costs of the product. Thus the choice of Cost Driver affects the accuracy of calculating product costs, in that it determines which products are relatively over- and undercosted.

We start this design choice with costs per ACP, broken down into a number of activity centres. We know from step 3 whether costs have been assigned by direct measurement or allocation. For example, if the setup costs of the above-mentioned machine classes resulted from *allocation*, using the allocation base "number of setup hours" – by means of which "ACP – machine class I" and "ACP – machine class II" were formed in step 3 – then in step 5, where we aim at an allocation by product, we can select another allocation base (driver), e.g. "number of setups". Cooper says about this:

"For the activity "setup", the cost drivers "number of setup hours" or "number of setups" might be considered. The driver "number of setups" assumes that each setup consumes the same amount of resources, irrespective of the product being setup, while the driver "number of setup hours" assumes that the consumption of resources varies by product, depending on the time it takes to set up the machines. Again, the choice of cost driver of second-stage allocation bases determines the level of distortion introduced into reported product costs.

The advantage of the two-stage procedure over a single-stage procedure is that different measures of resource consumption can be used at each stage. For example, the driver "number of setup hours" can be used in the first stage and the driver "number of setups" in the second stage. Having two stages is frequently beneficial, because the information that is available about the consumption of resources by center is often different from that available by product.[30]

30. It is this example which the numerical illustration in Appendix B is based on.

For example, setup personnel might log their time spent in each center but not on each product. Using the allocation bases "number of setup hours" in the first stage allows the system to capture some of the differences in resource consumption by center even though this information is not available at the product level."[31]

This type of allocation does *not* take place in the variability accounting system. The only costs which are recorded against the respective products (called product manufacturing objectives) are those which, via *direct* measurement – of the production factor quantities and services underlying the costs – are shown to be used/consumed *directly* by the respective products. Those costs which the ABC system allocates to individual products using volume-unrelated drivers are precisely characterized by being *indirect* in relation to the product units. However, this does not prevent the ex post calculation of product cost *outside* the accounts, using the variability accounting records as the source of information. Product costing was precisely one of the tasks which the variability accounting system was supposed to help solve.

That this does not take place in the variability accounting system is connected with Vagn Madsen's general assertion that each specific accounting task[32] demands a specific allocation base. This is exactly the problem with step 5. If, for example, the batch sizes of different production runs of a given finished product vary, then setup costs per unit in the batch will also vary. If the batch size of the finished product is constant, then the batch sizes of its various product parts can differ. Even in the event that all production batch sizes are constant, there will still be incongruities in order sizes between sales, production, and purchasing in the great majority of realistic cases. If the main target of our ex post calculation is the sales order, then we are forced to operate with an average per period for the other order sizes. In ex post calculations, the average will be those experienced in the accounting period, and in ex ante product costing, those expected in the budget period.

**Summary**

1. The level for aggregating actions into activities in step 1 of the ABC system is matched by the degree of detail in the cost-objectives dimension of the variability accounting system.
2. The determination of the degree of specification in step 2, where the aim is to be able to report costs for the various actions within an activity, will, in variability accounting, often be ensured via the simultaneously-recorded

31. Op. cit., pp. 40-41.
32. The four previously mentioned tasks: Accounting profit, product costing, control, and non-routine analyses.

department dimension. If the same department is involved in several kinds of actions within the same activity, then (as a rule) correspondingly more objectives accounts will have to be established in the variability accounting system. The necessary recording scope is the same for both ABC and variability accounting.

3. In ABC, Activity Cost Pools are established in step 3 by both "direct" and "indirect" measurement. In variability accounting, on the other hand, direct measurement forms the sole basis for the system's data. If direct measurement of the resource consumption of a specified objective is abandoned, therefore, the costs involved are placed at a higher-level – more aggregated – objective.
4. ABC's concept of "Activity Centres" (step 4) corresponds to variability accounting's department dimension, though with the important difference that, in the former, there is no hierarchy in the cost recordings.
5. Cost drivers form the basis for – in step 5 – allocating the costs of the various ACPs to the products. Such a distribution does not take place at all *in* variability accounting. Step 5's product calculations in particular become less informative in cases of changing or incongruent order sizes in purchasing, production, and sales, if the ex post calculation is carried out per product unit, but this is also true in the case of the product level alone.

## 2.2. The Problem Within the Original Activity-Based Costing System

In this chapter, we will be taking a closer look at the problem raised at the end of the previous chapter, but from a somewhat different angle. This problem stems from the fact that the ABC system's ex post calculations are a function of actual activity during the accounting period, thus making it difficult to use this information as a basis for decision-making. The problem is illustrated in an example using sets of variability accounts. The illustration builds on the setup costs example in chapter 2.1.

As previously mentioned, an intrinsic feature of the variability accounting system is that a given cost is placed as far down the objectives hierarchy as a non-arbitrary allocation allows. However, in the event that two or more setup objectives are desired, the problem of exactly where to place them in the objectives hierarchy crops up. There are several possibilities here:

**Example**

The three figures below (figures 9-11) show different recording depths. The further down the objectives hierarchy it is wished to assign setup costs in the accounts structure, the more detailed the measurement required. A position as shown in figure 11, for example, requires the recording of which specific product setup is being carried out for, while figure 10 merely demands a

**Figure 9:** Placing setup costs as adjacent objectives to product groups.

- setup - machine class I
- setup - machine class II
- product group A
  - product $A_1$
  - product $A_2$
  - product $A_3$
- product group B
  - product $B_1$
  - product $B_2$

**Figure 10:** Placing setup costs as immediately superjacent objectives to products *groups*.

- product group A
  - setup - machine class I
    - product $A_1$
    - product $A_2$
    - product $A_3$
- product group B
  - setup - machine class II
    - product $B_1$
    - product $B_2$

**Figure 11:** Placing setup costs as immediately superjacent objectives to individual products.

- product group A
  - setup - machine class I
    - product $A_1$
  - setup - machine class I
    - product $A_2$
  - setup - machine class I
    - product $A_3$
- product group B
  - setup - machine class II
    - product $B_1$
  - setup - machine class II
    - product $B_2$

recording of the product group.[33] On the other hand, figure 9 requires no identification of either product or product group, only a recording of the machine class on which the setups are carried out.

It's worth noting that the examples in figures 10 and 11 assume a one-to-one relationship between machine class and products – i.e. that product group A is always produced on machine class I and product group B always on machine class II. If this were not the case, however, then the two objectives hierarchies illustrated in figures 10 and 11 would have to be changed to those in figures 10b and 11b.

**Figure 10b:** Placing setup costs as immediately superjacent objective to product groups, as a function of processing site.

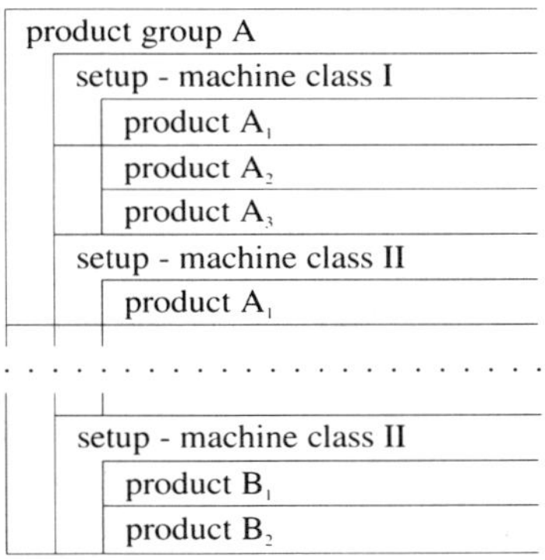


**Figure 11b:** Placing setup costs as immediately superjacent objectives to individual products, as a function of processing site.

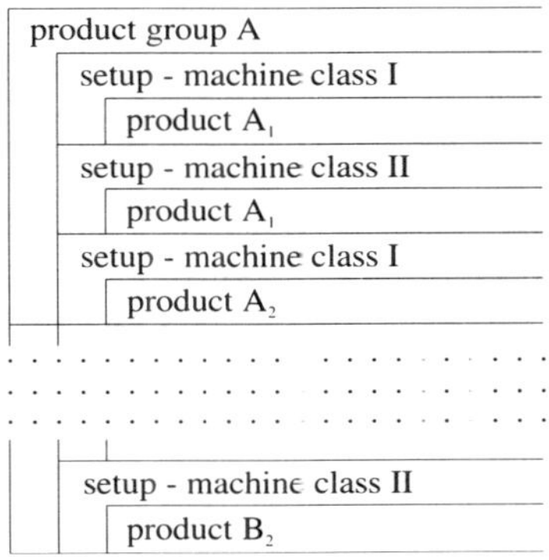


This type of illustration – which is that employed by Vagn Madsen – has a shortcoming here in that one gets the impression that now twice the number of account numbers have to be established in the objectives dimension in order to handle direct product costs. This is not necessary, however, since the type of machine class can be seen from the simultaneously registered cross-referenced department dimension. In the situations shown in figures 10b and 11b,

33. Actually, this is not necessary, since the machine-class designation – in this version of the example – is sufficient, inasmuch as the position of the cost account presupposes that machine class I is only used for product group A, and machine class II solely for product group B.

it must also be expected that, in the majority of realistic cases, the direct costs of producing a single unit in the batch – i.e. costs recorded under the respective product objectives as subjacent objectives of the "product manufacturing objective" – are different, a function of whether production takes place on the one or the other machine class.

In the following, this example will be used to show that product- and product-unit costs, which are the end result (step 5) of *calculations in the ABC system, are a function of the actual utilization of the means of production during the accounting period, and are unsuitable for purposes of price-determination, ex post calculation of product costs, and control, and at times directly misleading.*

Assume, as illustrated in figures 10b and 11b, that all the firm's products can be made on both machine classes, and that machine class II is newer than machine class I, thus being less resource-demanding to retool and, as regards direct product costs, cheaper to run. In this situation, the estimated costs per manufactured product unit for the accounting period will be a function of the actual utilization of the two machine classes.

A rational utilization of machine capacity would dictate using machine class II *first*, only bringing machine class I into use if capacity needs overstretched the capacity of class II. If this is the actual way the capacities are utilized, then the ABC system will show higher product unit costs the greater the actual capacity utilization.

A starting point in an average which is dependent on capacity utilization is unsuitable for ex post calculations of product unit costs. One needs to be able to start from *single* elements of the product's manufacture in this type of calculation. In the example, this means the possibility for carrying out ex post calculations of the extent to which the setup costs of the two machine classes and the direct costs per product per machine class are at more or less the same level as the expected – ex-ante-calculated – costs.

For control purposes, the aim of which is to search for explanations of actual behaviour and, if desired, individual responsibility, the same single elements are needed. Furthermore, we also need information to help evaluate whether machine class II has been used optimally – i.e. at a maximum in the example.

Finally, it also applies to price determination. It is a well-known fact that the optimum sales price cannot be determined on the basis of the firm's costs of producing the product concerned, even if it apparently seems that way in practice. The actual starting point is a knowledge – more or less certain – of market-price sensitivity, combined with a knowledge of the product's short- and long-term marginal costs. The latter are dependent on the composition and total expected scale of production, however. But the data already recorded in the accounts can only be helpful to us here – expressed within the framework of the example – by forming the basis for updating our ex ante calculations of the setup costs of the two machine classes and the resources consumed in the production of a single unit on the respective capacities. It is total expected demand at the alternative price levels, combined with a knowledge of the cost efficiency of producing on the two capacities which determines whether machine class I is to be used, and to what extent.

**Summary and conclusion**

It has been shown that, if the firm has several manufacturing capacities and production methods with different efficiencies at its disposal, the ABC system's ex post calculations are a function of actual capacity utilization. As a basis for solving price-determination-, ex post calculation-, and control tasks, this is unsuitable, since, in order to update the firm's ex ante calculations, all we need here – as far as costs are concerned – are the individual elements (the respective activities) in the products' manufacture.

If we pair the above with the conclusion from step 5 in chapter 2.1, *it follows that the ABC system's product unit costs are a function of the actual order sizes used in purchasing, production, sales and distribution, and of the actual capacity demand and capacity allocation over the accounting period. In relation to the primary task of the ABC system, this is inappropriate.*

## 2.3. Cost Registration versus Utilization of Cost Information

The previous examples of recording depth in a variability hierarchy will be used in this chapter to point out an essential difference between ensuring non-arbitrariness in cost recording and ensuring non-arbitrariness in the use of these costs for purposes of profitability analysis and as information on which management's economic decision-making is based.

In variability accounting, the attraction of recording lies in the possibility it creates for analysing the efficiency of carrying out the respective objectives through a study of their costs per unit of the variability factor. This information can help the firm *adjust its expectations* of the costs of carrying out a given objective, or to *motivate it to search for alternative*, less resource-demanding ways of achieving the same effect. Furthermore, these costs form the basis of stepped contribution margin layouts. Here, arbitrary allocations of costs by revenue segments are *not* carried out if these are relatively fixed[34] vis-à-vis the segment concerned. These costs then appear as *common costs* of that segment. Instead of allocating these costs, the income segments are summated, to which the costs are then relatively variable. An example of such a stepped contribution margin layout is shown in figure 12.

The information basis of the stepped contribution margin layout in figure 12 corresponds to the recording scope of figure 10b. But it is still a dubious source of information on which to base product decisions, or analyse the profitability of the various products.

**Figure 12:** Stepped contribution margin layout based on a recording scope corresponding to figure 10b.

| | Product $A_1$ | Product $A_2$ | Product $A_3$ | Product $B_1$ | Product $B_2$ |
|---|---|---|---|---|---|
| Revenue | aaa | aaa | aaa | aaa | aaa |
| Product-direct costs on machine class II | bbb | bb | | bbb | b |
| Product-direct costs on machine class I | | c | ccc | | cc |
| CM 1 | ddd | dd | d | ddd | dd |
| | | EEEEEEE | | | EEEEE |
| Setup costs on machine class I | | f | | | ff |
| Setup costs on machine class II | | ggg | | | gg |
| CM 2 | | RRRRR | | | RRR |

If the loss of efficiency of using machine class I rather than machine class II is the same for all five products, then from an economic point of view, it does not matter which product is made on which machine class. But it does matter as regards the information value of the relevant contribution margin layout. Products and product groups which are mainly produced on the least efficient machinery appear relatively less profitable than they actually are. This is due to the fact that, in relation to the relevant economic calculation, the *extra* costs of producing on machine class I are allocated among the products arbitrarily.

34. Cf. the discussion on the relativized use of the concepts fixed and variable in chapter 2.2.

In the situation outlined above, the relevant information for managerial-economic analysis is as in figure 12b.

In figure 12b, the product-direct extra costs are allocated first to the products which have yielded the lowest contribution margin before setup costs – CM I – per machine hour on machine class II, and to an extent which corresponds to actual total machine-hour utilization of machine class I. Similarly, the extra setup costs of machine class I are allocated to the products which have the lowest CM III per machine hour.

**Figure 12b:** Managerial-economic contribution margin analysis, based on a recording scope corresponding to figure 10b.

| | Product $A_1$ | Product $A_2$ | Product $A_3$ | Product $B_1$ | Product $B_2$ |
|---|---|---|---|---|---|
| Revenue | aaa | aaa | aaa | aaa | aaa |
| Product-direct costs on machine class II | bbb | vbb | vvv | bbb | vvb |
| Product-direct ***extra*** costs on machine class I | yy | y | | | y |
| CM II | zzd | zdx | xxx | ddc | zdx |
| Setup costs on machine class II | gg | gg | gg | g | gg |
| CM III | hhh | hh | hhh | h | hh |
| ***Extra*** costs of setup on machine class I | ii | i | | | i |
| CM IV | RR | RR | RRR | RR | R |

The recording basis outlined in figure 10b, does not enable us to distinguish the setup *costs* of individual products. As far as the *number* of setups is concerned, we could either have recorded number of setups per machine class (the variability factor would then correspond to the recording depth of the costs), or number of setups per product per machine class (higher degree of specification than setup costs). The latter is the most realistic here, because in order to record direct product costs per product, we would have to identify batches of completed production runs per product. Consequently, we can take advantage of the fact that the number of production batches per product corresponds to the number of setups per product. On the basis of this information, therefore, the best we can do is to assume that setup costs – given the machine class – are independent of the product for which setup is being carried out.[35] Our recordings therefore enable us to calculate the average historical setup costs of product group A and product group B per machine class – in other words, four historical figures. It is these figures that are behind figure 12b's division of setup costs into setup costs of machine class II and the *extra* costs of setup and changeover of machine class I. *The way figure 12b is constructed will thus help the firm weigh up the economic alternatives of utilizing these two machine classes.*[36]

The analysis results in the following needed clarification concerning recording in the variability accounting system and the use of these records for analysis and control purposes *outside* the accounts:

In variability accounting, a simultaneous recording of the consumption's type of production factor, department, and cost objectives is carried out at the time of resource consumption. In the department and objectives dimensions, consumption is recorded in accordance with the depth of recording obtained by direct measurements (including self-assessed time consumption). The less the depth of specification (for the machine dimension: machines en bloc, machine class, or individual machine; and for the product dimension: products en bloc, product group, or product), the more aggregated departments and objectives must be, since no allocation of cost consumption against departments and objectives, based on indirect measurements (allocation bases), is carried out. This ensures that there is no arbitrary allocation in the recording of resource *consumption. As the example shows, however, this does not automatically ensure a non-arbitrary basis in relation to the use of the information for analytic and decision-making purposes.* However, careful analysis of the data in the variability accounts prior to using them as input in managerial-economic calculations is a potential way of overcoming the problem.

If we return to figure 12b, the analysis can be used in the following argumentation:

If we assume that those costs recorded as product and direct setup costs are such as to be reversible – either automatically or dispositively – with the production and setup scale respectively, then all results, in the form of CM IV,

35. The use of updated ex ante calculations, as shown in appendix B, is also a possibility here, but is omitted in the interests of simplification. That standard costs can be involved as an allocation base at this point, and not earlier, is due to the fact that here we are dealing with the use of the variability accounting system's data *outside* the accounts.

36. A parallel to this problem complex occurs in cases where the firm has both in-house production as well as outside suppliers of identical components and/or finished goods at their disposal.

should be positive. If they are not, then those products which display a negative CM IV should be targeted for selective marketing measures, including possible elimination from the firm's product programme.

At least two reasons would preclude elimination, the first being the launching of the product on the market via low introductory prices, and the second that the firm presumes interdependencies between sales of the product in question and the other products. A more thorough examination of the latter argument requires another form of analysis, however, one which takes a starting point in another specification of total revenue, e.g. revenue per customer/customer group, or distribution channel.

On the other hand, carrying out such a contribution margin analysis means that we cannot at the same time maintain the differentiation in figure 12b between productions on the old and the new machinery. In the contribution margin analysis of customers, for example, we would have to employ a per unit cost figure which corresponds to average product-direct costs and average setup costs of actual (in the case of the ex post analysis of accounts) or expected/planned (in the case of budget- and non-routine considerations) capacity utilization and batch size. But these averages are still not the same as that produced by a direct calculation based on existing records. If, for example, 70% of production takes place on the new machinery and 30% on the old, then the relevant average costs per unit of each product are a correspondingly weighted average for the product and direct setup costs, respectively. This necessity is born of the fact that, under all normal circumstances, there is no congruence in the number of product units in sales and in production. Vagn Madsen has never advocated disallowing arbitrary allocations either. On the contrary, he has emphasized that they must not occur in the basic records, because the allocation bases must be determined by the purpose of the analysis, and therefore lie outside the cost accounts, though with these as source.

Now it could be claimed that, within the framework of this simple example, it actually is possible, in the customer contribution margin analysis, to handle both the incongruence between customer orders and production orders and the difference in costs between producing on the new and the old machinery. This is accomplished (on the basis of the aforementioned customer contribution analysis, which is therefore indispensable) by making the least-contributory customers shoulder all the extra direct costs of producing on the old machinery, plus a similar amount of the extra costs of setup on the old machinery, in proportion to the quantity demanded and the production batch size employed. By this means, the analysis layout will once again support the kind of information needed in decision-making. However, one must be aware of the difficulties of carrying out such a correct *incremental* analysis outside the framework of a simple example. In business practice one is faced with several relevant segment analyses – segmented by product, customer, geographical area, distribution channel, order size, etc. – which interact in a complex way in generating both revenue and costs.

The product- and customer analysis – two examples of a whole variety of segment analyses – also shows that there is a *considerable* difference between the hierarchy in the stepped contribution margin layout and the constructed hierarchies in the cost accounts.

The starting point in the stepped contribution margin layout is the chief aim of the analysis problem – whether it be an analysis of the profitability of products or customers, etc. – in relation to which it is determined which cost objectives are common and which are segment-direct at each step in the analysis hierarchy. If a cost objective – at a given step in the contribution margin layout – is common for several income segments, then, as previously stated, the calculated contribution margins of all the steps up to this one are aggregated. In this way, the position of a cost objective in the stepped contribution margin layout will be a function of – be relative to – the analysis problem. We characterize this by saying that *the stepped contribution margin layout's hierarchy is problem-determined or problem-derived.* Furthermore, it is worth noting that these contribution margin layouts occur *outside* the variability accounting system since this is a 100% cost accounting system.

*On the other hand, the hierarchies in the variability accounts' cost objectives are solely natural hierarchies.* As described in chapter 2.2, the hierarchies in the objectives dimension are defined by means of the relative definition of fixed and variable resource consumption. Far from all resource consumptions have such a relatively fixed/variable relationship to each other, however. In these cases, we say that, in a recording sense, the objectives are *functionally independent.* Advertising costs, for example, are functionally independent of the organisation of production. *These functionally independent areas appear as adjacent objectives in the system of variability accounts.* It is the ranking of these adjacent objectives which takes place in the stepped contribution margin layout.

As we shall see in chapter 3, this ranking depends not only on the aforementioned primary analysis problem, but also on the time horizon applied.

**Summary**

A system of non-arbitrary cost recordings, as in variability accounting, does not *automatically* protect against arbitrariness in the analysis of revenue-/cost segments (contribution segments) and in managerial-economics calculations. In principle, the processing of the system's basic data – outside the system – does allow these problems to be avoided. In practice, however, it is subject to a number of limitations, due to the fact that several relevant segments – e.g. products, customers, geographical areas, distribution channels, and order sizes – interact in a complex way in revenue creation and in their effect on costs, thus making *analytically correct* incremental analyses more difficult.

Chapter 2.3 concludes by drawing attention to the difference between the hierarchy principle used in variability accounting's objectives dimension and the stepped placing of costs in the contribution-analysis hierarchies. The hierarchies differ in that the former are *natural* hierarchies – and are thus unchanging with an unchanged recording scope – while the latter are a function of the aim of the analysis, and are thus *problem-determined.*

## 2.4. The Scope of Costs in the ABC System

So far, the question of which costs form part of the ABC system has not been addressed. All the conclusions up to now concerning the modus operandi of the ABC system have therefore been arrived at independently of the system's delimitation of costs. What these costs are, and the scale of activity on which their allocation is based, is discussed below. In the following chapter, we look at how the two systems deal with the relationship between consumption costs and opportunity costs.

We saw from the earlier description of the variability accounting system that it includes a period's entire actual resource consumption, *excluding depreciations*. The reason for keeping all forms of depreciations outside variability accounting records is that it is not possible to indicate a variability factor for this type of cost. It is worth noting, however, that the quantitative utilization (measured in time units) of the equipment is described in the factor input statistics in the usual three dimensions (cf. figure 2). For the other factors of production, the resource consumption is evaluated at standard prices, or at actual purchase prices.[37]

37. Irrespective of whether standard prices are chosen or not, the aim of the variability accounting system is to get as close as possible to the period's actual purchase prices. In other words, that the system makes use of budget prices (standard prices) does not mean it regards them as "norms" or "ideals", only that it wants to simplify cost recording by using the same prices as those used in the budget. As a result, any deviation between actual and budgeted prices is detected at the point of purchase of the resources, as opposed to the time of consumption.

The scope of costs and their evaluation basis in the ABC system is not discussed in other than general terms in Cooper's article series:

"In an activity-based system, the cost of a product is the sum of the costs of all activities required to manufacture and deliver the product."[38]

Elsewhere,[39] Cooper and Kaplan mention two – and only two – important exceptions to the principle that a product's cost is the sum of all the costs of a period. These are the research and development (R&D) costs of completely new products, and the costs of idle or unemployed capacity. The R&D costs of changing and improving the existing product range are therefore included in ABC's product costs – presumably via their consumption of engineering design capacity. As far as depreciations are concerned, this limitation means that the period's depreciations – which, for want of anything else are assumed to be the same amount as in the financial statement – are allocated to the products with the minimum amount per machine hour, which results from a calculation based on maximum capacity utilization.

Though both reasonable and correct, these exceptions do not cover all situations, just as the reasons for them can be problematical or wanting. We shall therefore take a closer look at them. This discussion takes place in light of the fact that economic data about these two groups of resources are included in a number of different information systems, each of which cover a particular information need.[40] The systems can well be integrated – in the sense of sharing a common database – but the processing of the data must necessarily take place in accordance with the information need they serve. Thus these systems may be criticized for the fact that their data processing is inadequate, or that the data is being used outside their sphere of application, but not for the fact that the data processing is different from system to system.

38. Cooper, "The Rise of Activity-Based Costing – Part One: What is an Activity-Based Cost System?", p. 46.
39. Cooper & Kaplan, "Measure Cost Right: Make the Right Decisions", pp. 101-102, and Kaplan, "One Cost System Isn't Enough", p. 65.
40. Amongst others, these systems include:
    - Investment evaluation systems: containing different types of capital budgeting techniques (e.g. NPV, IRR) and/or more general cost/benefit systems.
    - Investment monitoring systems: data collection and follow-ups of whether the approval criteria for investments and expected consequences of them actually are fulfilled, corrective measures being set in motion if this is not the case.
    - Accounting statements and -budgets: containing statements on actual and expected profit and loss, balance, and cash-flow consequences of the period's activities.
    - ABC's product calculations: inspirational basis for changed policies and behaviour, including price policy. (Explained and further elaborated later in chapter 2.5, 4, and 5).

For both cost groups, the main argument given is that they represent "investments in the future". Or, put another way, for R&D costs of new products and deliberate investment in surplus plant capacity, *the investments in question are first expected to show a profit in the long term.*

If "investments in the future" can justify excluding these costs from the allocation of costs to existing products, then a lot of other costs could also be excluded. These could, for example, include major – possibly multi-period – constructions of buildings and major equipment, extensive renovations of the same, and the costs of establishing major administrative and/or intangible assets. What all of these cost groups have in common is that they are examples of "cost objectives" which, in Vagn Madsen's variability accounting system, appear as "investment objectives", as distinct from "operating objectives".[41] In periodic reporting of profits to management – note that we are now talking about one of the variability accounting tasks which is solved outside the basic recording system – the investment objectives are characterized by being excluded from calculations of the period's product contribution (i.e. profit before depreciations, interest, tax).[42] On this point, then, it would seem possible to bridge the differences between the two systems via – as regards the ABC system – a stricter adherence to the "investment in the future" argument. Agreement ends, however, when we delve into the structure of the product-profit reporting format, since in variability accounting it takes the form of the stepped contribution hierarchy shown in chapter 2.3, and not full-cost product- or product-unit costs.[43]

However, a much simpler explanation for keeping the R&D costs of new products out of the ABC system's product calculation – which Cooper and Kaplan do not mention, however, – should be that it is *impossible* to find an allocation base or driver which describes any sensible relation between these resources and the existing product portfolio. This applies whether it just concerns an allocation mechanism or an actual driver for expressing a cause-and-effect relationship in a causal or final sense. Cooper and Kaplan's assertion – that the profitability of R&D costs of new products must be evaluated

41. Cf. the note to the variability accounting chart of accounts reproduced in supplement 1.
42. Specifically, by capitalizing the costs of the various investment objectives, and later deducting them as depreciations in the income statement to arrive at net profit. The depreciations start from the point at which the assets are taken into use, and must therefore be expected to have a revenue-increasing or cost-saving effect, and a length of time for calculating the depreciation corresponding to the expected duration of the effect.
43. As can be seen from chapter 4, this difference has been greately narrowed with the latest developments in activity-based theory.

through a "life-cycle-costing" investment calculus system, and not in a historical and budgeted income statement which immediately writes these of as costs of the period, or via additions to product costs – is not in itself incorrect, but as an argument in the complex of problems surrounding product calculation, it is irrelevant. The argument reflects a confusion of the separate information needs served by different information systems.

The reason that Cooper and Kaplan give for the absence of product allocation for unemployed machine capacity is the familiar and correct one that any other basis for attributing costs would yield distortions due to fluctuations in activity. Applied to depreciations, other types of standard costs (e.g. costs based on normal or budgeted capacity utilization), or actual costs, the consequence would be a fluctuation in the ex-ante- and ex-post-calculated product costs, brought about by corresponding changes in expected and actual activity levels – in other words, the lower the activity the higher the product costs, and vice versa, which is completely misleading in the case of external price determination. That Cooper and Kaplan also reject using other depreciation schemes in the annual financial statement is irrelevant as far as the ABC calculation is concerned, partly because ABC calculations embrace a lot of other costs than those which, from a functional point of view, are production costs (which is why, for this reason alone, they are not comparable with the product cost calculation in the profit and loss statement), and partly due to a mix-up of information systems.

The two above-mentioned cost groups are the only exceptions to full product cost allocation in Cooper and Kaplan's account. I would include a number of others, however, over and above those already mentioned as corresponding to variability accounting's investment objective. *The criterion for exclusion would be that they are capacity costs with little or no absolute divisibility and which at the same time are not directly involved in the taking and carrying out of orders.* Those capacities which are not involved in the chain of activities starting from the taking of an order, through production, to final delivery are characterized (in the variability accounting system) in being attributed variability factors which are *independent* of the scale of activities in purchasing, production and sales, together with their support functions. By this, those costs which, in variability accounting's department dimension are placed at the upper part of the hierarchy, and in the objectives dimension appear under general administration costs or as marketing costs (which logically come before order-taking), are excluded from the product-cost calculation. Also, according to this criterion, depreciation on buildings would not be included in the product calculation either, since this capacity has no (or little) divisibility and, at the same time, cannot be attributed any load factor unit which is related to the activities involved in carrying out the sale, production and delivery of an order.

Maximum capacity utilization is suggested as the scale of activity at which the remaining cost objectives within the "operations objectives" category are allocated to products, which is in line with Cooper and Kaplan's starting point for machine depreciations. This guideline for selecting the scale of activity means not only estimating the maximum number of load factor units per unit of capacity (possibly converted to capacity utilization units where the capacity – here primarily consisting of salaried employees – is involved in several types of activity), but also how much each product-/order type uses the respective activities up to their completion. This proposal is probably not inconsistent with Cooper and Kaplan's intentions concerning the ABC calculation, even though they have not been explicit on this score. The suggestion also results from the fact that, at this point, I am trying to be faithful to the declared main aim of the ABC calculation, which is ostensibly to improve product calculation in support of external price determination.

The above-mentioned main aim of the ABC calculation leads to the following comments:

Firstly, it shows that it is irrefutably the ex ante calculation and not the potential ex post calculation per product-order type which counts.

Secondly, it must be emphasized that it is solely an *aid* to price determination, and thus not a basis from which a mechanical extrapolation of the external price can be inferred, inasmuch as the cost calculations do not take price sensitivity or competitive conditions in the market into account. A simple and constant mark-up percentage of calculated product costs is therefore never likely to be the most rational reaction.

Thirdly, the product cost calculation must be made transparent as regards employed production factors. No such transparency results from Cooper's five design choices. Thus step 2 and 4 of these design choices merely showed that the depth of reporting was solely concerned with a greater or lesser degree of specification of the activities involved – in step 2 as far as particularization of "actions" was concerned, and in step 4 concerning contributory "activity centres". The importance of transparency in the ex ante calculation becomes clear when it is remembered that periodic adjustments of selling prices are often necessary in practical price policy, and that this must take place within the limitations imposed both by the market and the firm's cost structure. Only via transparency in the production factors can the product cost calculation serve as a first informative step to cost reversibility, because this attribute is connected to the input factor dimension. As chapters 1 and 1.1 showed, such transparency is ensured in this interpretation of the variability accounting system. Furthermore, this transparency is crucial for the calculation policy – which builds on a combination of consumption costs and opportunity costs – discussed in chapter 5.

**Summary**

The ABC system includes all the firm's costs in the product calculation except those of unused machine capacity and the R&D costs of completely new products, since both represent "investments in the future" and not costs of current products. The same reason is used in this chapter to argue for excluding all other investment costs, which, in the variability accounting system, proves to correspond to excluding costs under the investment objective, since these are precisely characterized by the fact that they are not expected to have revenue- or cost-saving effects during the period in which they are incurred. This chapter also argues in favour of leaving out of the product calculation those costs of the various types of capacity which show no or only little absolute divisibility and which at the same time are not directly involved in the taking and carrying out of orders.

Finally, transparency in *production factor costs* is desirable in the product-cost calculation, since a sine qua non of rational price adjustment is knowledge of cost reversibility, which is precisely an attribute of the production factor dimension.

### 2.4.1. Consumption Costs versus Opportunity Costs

In both the ABC and the variability accounting systems, a period's resource consumption is evaluated at consumption cost as opposed to opportunity cost. Implicit in this is that it costs the same to *use* a factor of production as it has cost to *procure* it. In the variability accounting system, however, this does not apply to the use of fixed assets, since depreciations are excluded. This chapter explains briefly why the two systems do not contain opportunity costs, followed by a demonstration of the fact that, despite this, the factor input and cost statistics of the reformulated variability accounting system contain all the necessary and – with two exceptions – sufficient *internal* ex post data for the calculation of opportunity costs.

The reason that the variability accounting system does not contain opportunity costs[44] is that it would conflict with the pluralistic nature of the

44. There are two uses of opportunity cost in the literature: The one – which we call the narrow definition – defines it as "the largest foregone contribution margin from a chosen course of action". The other – the expanded definition - includes the above, but with the addition of the avoidable costs of carrying out the action. The narrow definition is used here.

system. It will be remembered that one of the identified tasks of variability accounting is to furnish some of the data on which the solution of non-routine tasks is based, but that the calculation of opportunity costs (one of the non-routine calculations) itself takes place *outside* the system. Since it is precisely in connection with the consideration of alternative causes of action that opportunity costs are calculated – no alternatives, no sacrifice – it is only logical that the system does not estimate the opportunity cost of resource consumption. Instead, the system records those consumption costs which form the basis of the calculation of avoidable costs, and which are a necessary – but not sufficient – element in an overall comparison of alternatives.

It is easy to see why the ABC system does not contain opportunity costs. The declared principal aim of the ABC system – in its original version, which is the one discussed here – is, as previously stated, to form the basis of external price determination. Calculating opportunity costs requires external sales prices as an input in the calculation process, however. Even though the whole process surrounding the determination of products' avoidable costs, capacity needs, and external sales price can be carried out iteratively, it does not fundamentally change this fact. Including opportunity costs in the ABC system would therefore have the effect of reversing the input and output of the calculation. (Notwithstanding, it is a step in this direction which is the subject of chapter 5).

To substantiate the claimed interaction between opportunity costs and variability accounting recordings, it is necessary to take a closer look at capacity costs[45] – excluding depreciation on fixed assets. As far as these costs are concerned, we find that the underlying production factors show a wide spectrum of time horizons – both acquisition and discharge horizons, by which is meant the period of time between the decision to increase or decrease resource availability and the economic consequences of that decision. In further discussions of the importance of this, we limit ourselves to the *discharge* horizons of already acquired resources. To begin with, we focus on the resources used in the firm's various support functions in purchasing, production, and sales. Following this, we look at the resources used in the direct manufacture of products.

To recapitulate, Vagn Madsen defined a variability factor as a common quantitative factor with which costs – automatically or dispositively – vary approximately proportionately. According to the reformulation of variability accounting in chapter 1.1, however, a variability factor is a common

45. Depending on the discharge possibilities and policies of the individual firm, these also include operator wages.

quantitative factor with which *consumption/use* of the production factor input – monetary equivalent not included – varies approximately proportionately. In a decision situation – a consideration of alternative courses of action – concerning resource allocation, where the decision horizon is shorter than the discharge horizon, the costs of acquiring both these resources and their derived consumption costs are irrelevant, since the expenditures and costs concerned are irreversible. *However, the variability factor attributed to the cost objective in question will then appear as a measure of the utilization of the capacity concerned.* A not inconsiderable practical problem is next to determine the performance potential of available capacity. An initial estimate of historical "maximum practical capacity" could consist of a realistic standard cost (assessed at consumption costs) per unit of the variability factor, divided by the total costs recorded against the objective account in question.[46] However, it is not so easy to determine a realistic standard cost – and thus "maximum practical capacity" – for the support activities focused on here. Labour is the dominant factor of production here, but labour productivity is notoriously difficult to determine with any great degree of precision. A productivity or intensity adjustment is therefore a possibility. Any dispositive savings, or incremental costs, appear only later, however. Put another way, the number of activities can change in the short run, but not acquisition costs or derived consumption costs.[47] What is more crucial here, though, is to note that the above-mentioned standard consumption costs per unit of variability factor are unimportant as far as economic considerations connected to the decision situation are concerned. Only opportunity costs are important. These are not derivable from a historical cost account, but must appear as an element in the firm's contemplated alternative courses of action and planning for the future.

If we incline towards an interpretation of the variability factor as a measure of capacity consumption in the direct manufacture of products, then previous conclusions are not applicable without further qualification. It would be natural to think of the variability factor for the product manufacturing objective as being "number of produced units". But this is unsuitable in those cases where

46. Alternatively, the same capacity evaluation could be carried out on the quantitative – non-monetary – level alone, where the estimate is then related to consumption of time per activity.
47. The majority of these costs comprise what Riebel calls "Costs of readiness" (Bereitschaftskosten; see, for example, Riebel, *Einzelkosten- und Deckungsbeitragsrechnung*). The present discussion is not a dissociation of Riebel's assertion that these sorts of costs are a function of *expected* activity, and that they therefore cannot be evaluated or followed-up against actual activity. What we are looking for here – based on the body of experience contained in the accounts – is solely to determine the activity *potential*.

several different products are produced on the same equipment (e.g. machine classes). For this, we need a variability factor which can both measure equipment capacity and at the same time be a common term for the various "product objectives'" utilizations of this capacity. Böhm and Wille's concept of "Standard Belegungsstunden" (cf. chapter 1.1), which is a quantitative measure in time units, is a natural choice here.[48] Since the materials that go into the various products and components are different both in terms of quality and value, "Standard Belegungsstunden" would be a poor variability factor for these production factor costs. The same – though more unusually – could apply in the case of direct wages, which occurs in those cases where there is a difference in the number of direct wage hours per machine hour on the same machinery as a function of the product being made. The simultaneous recording of the type of production factor and cost objective serves us well here, since we can use the variability factor "number of produced units" per product for the combined materials/product objective, and "number of SBS" for direct machine performance costs (e.g. energy but not depreciation). As far as product-direct wages are concerned, the choice of variability factor depends – as indicated above – on whether these are machine-related only, or also product-related. Whether the consumption cost "direct wages" is at all relevant in the decision situation outlined above depends, as previously mentioned, on the decision horizon. If it is shorter than labour's underlying discharge horizon, then it is irrelevant, i.e. that labour appears as a capacity, and labour's opportunity cost is relevant. If the decision horizon is longer, then direct wages appear as a variable consumption cost. *In a decision-making context, the monetary equivalent of any production factor cannot be relevant as consumption cost and opportunity cost at the same time.*

It is precisely the breadth (number of adjacent objectives) and depth (number of subjacent objectives) in the recordings of variability factors and costs per objective which is important for the detail and realism which can be put into the firm's cost projections of contemplated courses of actions. In the real world, knowledge of resources, capacities, variability factors and costs, which is strictly localized within the organisation, exerts little influence on management's economic decisions.

The above account shows that the variability accounts' performance and cost statistics contain the necessary historical data for updating the firm's ex ante

48. An example which shows "Standard Belegungsstunden" (SBS) to be a quantitative measure in time units is that an increase in production intensity results in increased production of SBS per orthodox hour. The conceptualization can be found in Böhm & Wille, *Deckungsbeitragsrechnung und Optimierung*.

product calculation as regards costs and capacity utilization. Note that this also applies to the various support functions. Both are a sine qua non of a realistic economic evaluation of alternative courses of actions.

What the variability accounting system does *not* provide is information about the discharge horizons – and thus the degree of reversibility – of the various factors of production. As chapter 1.1 showed, however, it is relatively easy to enlarge the system to accommodate this information need. In order to carry out economic evaluations of alternative courses of actions involving opportunity costs, additional information in the form of the capacity needs of sales order stocks-in-hand is required – only free capacity is still subject to continued economic priority, of course. Information about sales order stocks is accessible in other of the firm's recording systems, but must in this connection be converted to a realistic expected capacity utilization, which is where the historical experience contained in variability accounting system comes in useful.

Obviously, we also need to know about market expectations, the reactions of competitors, etc., but these lie outside the scope of this discussion.

**Summary**

Both the ABC and variability accounting systems employ consumption costs rather than opportunity costs as a basis for cost evaluation. ABC has to by virtue of its chief aim of supporting external price determination, as an evaluation at opportunity cost would require the predetermination of a product's sales price, which was precisely the aim of the calculation. Variability accounting has to so as not to prejudice its multi-purpose character.

It is shown in this chapter that variability factors can be interpreted partly as a capacity load factor measure (of interest in considering opportunity costs) and partly as a factor explaining/forecasting the size of the objectives costs (of interest in considering consumption costs). The relevance of the one or the other interpretation depends on the length of the decision horizon vis-à-vis the disposition horizon (reversibility) of the factors of production.

Finally, it is argued that variability accounting's ex post factor input- and cost statistics – except, in particular, the discharge horizon of the resources – contains the internal data necessary for *updating* the firm's ex ante calculations, including both direct production activities and the support functions in purchasing, production and sales connected with them.

## 2.5. The Original ABC System: Conclusion and Potential

It can be seen from the above that there are a lot of conceptual similarities, but also considerable differences, between the ABC and variability accounting systems. This chapter presents a short summing up of the main points of the comparative analysis, followed by an indication of the potential, vis-à-vis variability budgeting, which I find is implicit in the ABC system as described here.

The conceptual similarities embrace "activities" and "objectives", "ACPs" and "cost objectives", and "Cost Drivers" and "variability factors".

**a. "Activities" and "objectives" – these *are* equivalent**

The "activities" of the ABC system are conceptually identical to the "objectives" of variability accounting, since an activity is typically described by its immediate objective.

**b. "ACP" and "cost objectives" – these *can* be equivalent if the ACP in question results from direct measurement**

As described previously, ACPs are formed by both direct and indirect measurement of the quantitative – non-monetary – factor consumption and factor use. *Indirect measurement is not a measurement at all*, but an allocation base which is used to allocate costs to smaller ACPs than those for which the consumption is (directly) measured. Here, therefore, indirect measurements are arbitrary allocation bases. It should be emphasized that the term arbitrary is not meant deprecatingly here, it is only a characteristic of the fact that the allocation does not follow a causal cause-and-effect principle. Despite this, it can still serve a purpose – in the sense "to help solve an accounting task" – in this case products' cost calculation. Such allocations do not occur *in* variability accounting.

One should be cautious about equating ACPs with cost objectives, even in cases where ACPs result from direct measurements. This is because, in the ABC system, there are no guidelines for limiting ACPs. We saw from the delimitation of the cost objectives that the quantitative consumption/utilization of production factors should vary approximately proportional with the activity under the objective concerned. There is therefore no reason why one and the same ACP cannot include cost of production factors whose consumption varies/does not vary with the scale of the activity concerned. This is shown most clearly by the fact that the pools – unlike the cost objectives – also contain depreciations.

### c. "Cost Drivers" and "variability factors" – the *intention* behind these is the same

The differences and similarities between cost drivers and variability factors are not easily described. There are two reasons for this: (i) Firstly, because Cooper uses the driver concept solely to describe products' utilization of the various activities, while the term "first stage allocation base" is used to describe the formation of ACPs, whether the pool in question results from an allocation or direct measurement; (ii) secondly, because to a certain extent the driver concept suffers from the same difficulties of interpretation as Vagn Madsen's original variability factor concept, i.e. is it a measure of resource input or activity output? What is indisputable, however, is that they are both quantitative, non-monetary factors.

The difficulty under point (ii) is especially due to the fact that Cooper's – and many others' – description of the ABC system relates solely to ex post accounting figures, at which point one has, in principle, the choice of choosing between both input and output factors as allocation base/driver. In future-oriented – ex ante – decisions, however, a starting point must be taken in the planned output of the various activities, while the necessary input resources are subsequently produced through an ex ante calculation.

In a variability framework, there are variability factors corresponding to both levels in Cooper's classification, though with the difference that the distinction between levels is lacking. The area corresponding to level 1 (stage 1, figure 5) contains such variability factors as "no. of purchasing orders", "no. of production orders", "no. of sales orders", "no. of suppliers", "no. of customer visits", "no. of product design changes", etc., each of which must be used to both explain and predict the resource input which has occurred and is expected (is budgeted) to occur in connection with the carrying out of the respective activities/objectives. Virtually the only variability factors corresponding to the ABC system's product drivers at level 2 (stage 2, figure 5) appear in the variability accounting system's "product-manufacturing objective", and the majority of these are, in ABC terminology, "volume drivers", but, as previously described, batch costs also appear here. Costs which are indirect in relation to the "product manufacturing objective" are, of course, recorded in other objectives which have their own variability factors. Examples of such variability factors are mentioned above, and are characterized by being almost exclusively "volume-*un*related".

On this basis, it must be concluded that, although there are slight differences of meaning between variability factors and drivers, the fundamental intention behind and grounds for their use are the same, namely to establish other quantitative output measurements for explaining resource consumption, and with it costs, than volume-related ones.

There are also fundamental differences between the two systems, however. The differences pointed out here are connected with the different purposes the two systems were designed for. The variability accounting system was both conceived and framed as a basic recording system, to serve as a database for a series of information-processing tasks outside the system. The ABC system, on the other hand, was designed with the desire for an improved "full-cost" product calculation in mind.

These different purposes go a long way towards explaining the difference between the elements and principles of the two systems. These are that there is no cost hierarchy principle in the ABC system's principles for cost recording, that there is no explicit characterization of costs related to type of production factor, and that there is no simultaneous recording of the three dimensions of cost consumption: type of production factor, department, and cost objective. The omission of these three elements is intimately connected.

### d. Cost-recording hierarchy – potentially implicit in the ABC system's physical, non-monetary level

The main – bordering on the exclusive – interest in the "long-term" full-cost product unit calculation reduces interest in the cost hierarchy in the activity dimension – corresponding to the objectives dimension – which arises from interest in which resource consumptions are fixed or variable relative to obtaining and completing an order. There is an embryonic hierarchy principle in the system's physical, quantitative – non-monetary - level, however, even though it has no explicit form. This can be clearly seen in the above-mentioned "setup" costs. *That the hierarchy principle remains implicit is due to the lack of stringency in the presentation and discussion of what the "product" in "product costs" refers to*, since it can be variously interpreted as product units, individual product types, product groups, or entire product lines.

### e. A characterization of costs grouped according to type of production factor – a dimension lacking in ABC

The hierarchy principle is not applied to the corresponding economic evaluation, however, which, with the ABC system as starting point for price determination, precludes making allowance for the absolute and relative divisibility and degree of reversibility of the resources. The necessary – but not sufficient – condition for this would be for the system to incorporate a production factor dimension in the cost description at both the ex post and ex ante stage. Furthermore, if ex post recording takes place not in a basic multi-purpose accounting system (like variability accounts) but in a job-order costing system via a successive accumulation of the costs of carrying out the order's necessary activities, then this implies that the accumulation ought to take place per type of production factor.

### f. Simultaneous recording of production factor type, department, and cost objective – an attribute useful to ABC, which has been overlooked due to the research methodology employed

The research methodology used in the development of the ABC system is ostensibly[49] an inductive methodology employed in advanced business practice (primarily, but not exclusively, North American firms). The firms examined are more or less all well-established firms, or subsidiaries of such, which had their own cost-recording system, which, at the time of the study – or just before – had been found to be unsatisfactory, or directly misleading, in relation to the firm's "product-related"[50] decisions. Understandably, therefore, it was hoped to acquire better information for "product decisions" through adjustments to the established system or via ad hoc analyses primarily based on the recording scope of the existing cost system. By the latter is meant that the search for additional information is concentrated on the identification of volume-unrelated drivers (variability factors/load factor units) and to a lesser extent around further measurements and specifications of the resource- and cost consumption dimensions.[51] It is the difficulty of and slowness in overturning already-established systems, and the well-known acknowledgement of "different costs for different purposes" that form the background to Kaplan's assertion that "One Cost System Isn't Enough", later expanded to a "Four Stage Model of Cost System Design"[52], where the final evolutionary step (the fourth stage) consists of integrated cost systems which serve several information needs, based on interconnected databases. According to Kaplan, none of the examined firms has yet reached this stage. However, although not explicitly stated, there is no doubt that a satisfactory solution at this stage of development presupposes a rigorous distinction between data recording and

49. This can be seen in several places, amongst others in what could be described as Kaplan's research methodology "manifesto", cf. "The Evolution of Management Accounting", pp. 415-16.
50. Cooper and Kaplan's term. See, for example, "How Cost Accounting Distorts Product Costs".
51. A good example of this can be found in G.J. Beaujon & V.R. Singhal's description of the implementation of the original ABC system in General Motors, cf. "Understanding the Activity Costs in an Activity-Based Cost System".
52. These are both titles of articles by Kaplan. See bibliography for further references.

data manipulation, and that, as a minimum, the recording includes simultaneous identification of the resource consumptions' type of production factor, department, and cost objectives, but disposition horizon/reversibility and absolute divisibility of the resources used would also be welcome.[53]

We end this comparison between the original ABC system and the variability accounting system by taking another look at the question of arbitrary allocation bases.

As previously described, the ABC system *may* use allocation bases in establishing the system's Activity Cost Pools, but *certainly* uses them in attributing a number of these costs to products. Variability accounting, on the other hand, sticks only to what has been established by measurements of the resource consumption and a corresponding cost evaluation. Put another way, one could say that *a "two-stage-procedure" is ruled out in the variability accounting system. The expression "two-stage-procedure" implies an initial recording of the cost consumptions, which are later allocated.* But no allocations take place within the framework of the variability accounting system.

*On the other hand, it is worth noting that a basic accounting system such as variability accounting can deliver all the necessary data for the ABC system's calculations.* This is because the ABC's end result, in the form of product- or product unit costs, is produced exclusively on the basis of calculations – data manipulation – based on measurements kept accessible in separate accounts. The above-mentioned conclusion also applies to the depreciations in the ABC calculations, since, it will be remembered, variability accounting's quantitative – non-monetary – statistics include the capacities' utilization, characterized by the type of production factor, department, and cost objective, which is sufficient to allocate depreciations to products as long as the total amount of depreciation (which is a calculation and not a measurement) and the maximum capacity (an estimation, not a measurement) are known.

*In one important respect, the ABC system can be a good supplement to the use,* emphasized by Vagn Madsen, *of variability principles in budgetary planning and control.* To back up this view, therefore, a short account of Vagn Madsen's resource and cost control theory is outlined below.

According to Vagn Madsen, the most important control mechanism consists of organisational policies. Organisational policies:

53. On a very personal note, I would add that this also requires a higher degree of stringency in conceptualization within English-language cost theory and cost accounting theory.

"... contain the rules governing the organisation's activities and the limits imposed on the *individual elements* of the total activity programme. Policies, which are drawn up according to a strategy, partly reflect the organisation's interaction with its environment and partly the internal cooperation which this interaction necessitates." (My emphasis)[54]

To a large extent, the "individual elements" of the activity programme are the activities underlying the individual objectives. The policy concept, then, is the organisational equivalent to objectives which, as we have seen, is an accounting-/budgetary concept (an account). Not all policies have an objectives counterpart, however – e.g. the firm's financial policy (rules for: payment of suppliers, customers' terms of payment, investment of surplus liquidity, etc.), and the firm's inventories policy (size of stocks of raw materials, components, and finished goods). Individual policies cannot be formulated independently of and in isolation from each other, but must be harmonized, coordinated, and possibly ranked in importance. For example, policies for the time and guarantee of delivery to customers have an important effect on inventory policies of components and finished products and/or batch sizes in production (thus also for activities connected with setup and changeover, which in turn affects the complexity of organising the production flow), and, ultimately, for demands on suppliers for the time and guarantee of materials deliveries. Sales price policy, customer credit policy, product quality policy, sales service- and after sales service policies all affect sales expectations. It is the *combined effects* and interaction of these policies which determines the activities of the various cost objectives. However, there being no simple and transparent relationship between the effect of performing these activities and revenue creation – which is equivalent to saying that it is subjective and uncertain, and therefore characterized by many "value judgements"[55] – Vagn Madsen recommends that the means for controlling these activities should be policy formulations combined with budgetary control. Analyses of policy changes and their expected economic consequences for revenue creation and the scale of activity and costs occur, in accordance with this line of thought, in non-routine considerations (incremental economic calculations) outside the budget system, with the variability accounting system as one of several sources of reference. I basically agree with this point of view.

In practice, however, the problem is that the firm lacks any *criterion for deciding* which non-routine considerations to examine more closely, and both top- and department managers get too easily distracted by all the policy

54. Madsen, *Strategi og Budget,* p. 71.
55. Cf. the distinction between "Value Judgements" and "Factual Judgements" in H.A. Simon, *Administrative Behaviour.*

formulations and objectives.[56] *They become disoriented.* An analytical tool – "an orientation map" -, for identifying areas of necessary policies-changes and alternative methods of carrying out activities is needed. On this point, the basic idea of the ABC system is a potential help, though not in the version examined here.

These ideas are illustrated in figure 13, which is an expansion of figure 8:

**Figure 13**: The connection between Variability Factors, Drivers, and Sales Segments.

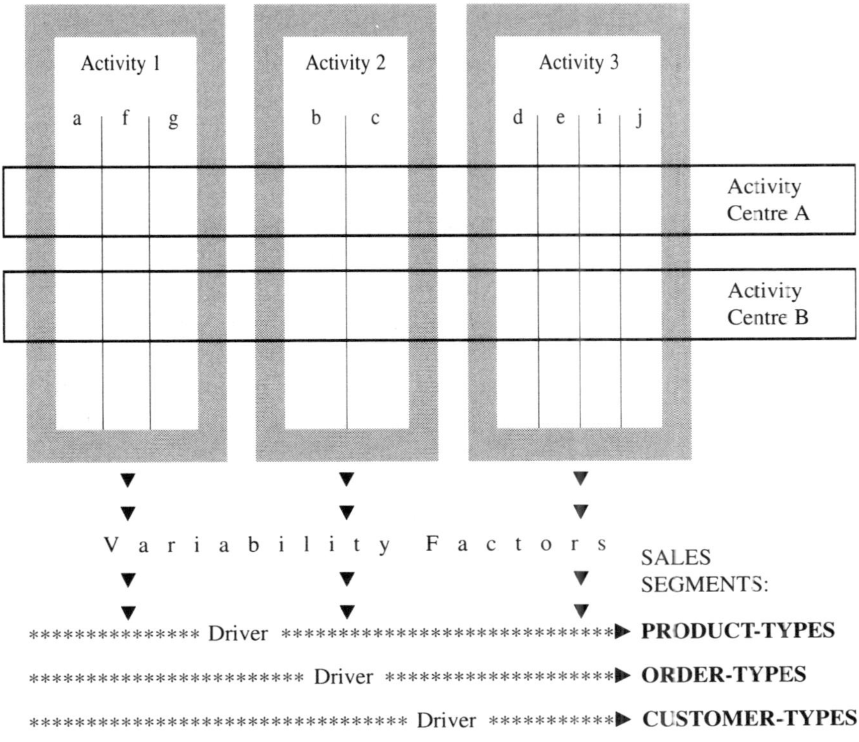


Note: The figure uses a changed content of the Driver concept. Explanation in accompanying text.

56. For documentation of the latter, see Thomas Polesie, *Ändamålsbudgettering - beskrivning och analys af tillämpninger.*

The figure operates with both variability factors and cost drivers, thus reflecting a changed conceptualisation – in this case concerning the concept "Cost Driver".

The variability factor remains the same. *The Driver concept is changed, and defined as a complex of variability factors which reflect the utilization and consumption of a sales segment on a number of the firm's activities.*

One possible basis for the formation of sales segments are the various products of the firm, which is what the ABC system has in mind, but another possibility than the typical subdivision into product lines could be sub-segments, in the form of standard/special products. A second basis for the formation of sales segments could be "order types" (whether large/small, rush/normal or tender/non-tender orders, etc.), and a third could be "customer type" (public/private, big/small, old/new, industry etc.).

Whichever criterion of classification – and thus segmentation of total revenue – is chosen as the primary (there can be several), and under which the others must explicitly be subordinated or subjugated, one is forced at some stage in the profit calculations of the segment in question to use arbitrary allocations of costs. This is partly due to the connection between the segments – all revenue thus originates from a certain customer type, who has placed a certain order, which consists of certain types of products, which is also why we cannot elevate one of these to be the main one for cost accounting – and partly because in this situation, a stepped contribution margin layout would be difficult to carry out, or only be a poor inspiration for eventual policy changes, since we would find a positive contribution in "the upper end" of all layouts irrespective of the segmentation criterion.

*Inspiration* is precisely the key word here, since what we are looking for is inspiration to determine the need for goal-oriented selective marketing measures in a segment. For example, rush orders lead to a lot of disruptions in production and organisation of production flow, and thus burden the firm with a number of specific extra activities (e.g. rescheduling, extra setups, etc.). Any estimate of these extra costs must start with the cost objectives per variability factor for activities connected with the rush order. The content of the order itself is of secondary importance in this context.

Of course, it would be tempting to conclude that you should not accept rush orders at all if they are so problematical. Solutions are rarely this simple, however. In fact, rejecting a rush order would be unwise unless it contained the least profitable products, ordered by the least profitable customers via the most costly distribution channels. If this were the case, you could cheerfully reject it.[57] In all other – and more realistic - situations, it is the firm's management who must cut through the very complex interconnectedness of segments and decide which product-, customer-, and order types to concentrate on.

One sort of analytic tool and means of orientation for these policy decisions seems to consist in regarding each segment as a "Cost Driver" and use the recordings in the variability accounts as a basis for the cost evaluation. One means of policy implementation is to let identified problem segments appear with explicit surcharges (cost supplements) in an operative ex ante calculation system, which serves as the basis for external price determination. Whether these surcharges should be assessed at consumption cost or opportunity cost is postponed to the concluding chapter.

Incidentally, the changes proposed here in the Driver concept brings it nearer to its original meaning of a "structural factor". More about this in the next chapter.

**Summary**

A number of similarities and differences have been identified between the original ABC system and the variability accounting system:

Similarities:

a. *"Activities" and "objectives"* ***are*** *equivalent concepts.*
b. *"ACP" and "costs objectives"* ***can*** *be equivalent if the ACP concerned results from direct measurement.*
   The lack of a more definitive conclusion is due to the fact that there is no explicit principle in ABC for attributing costs to an ACP.
c. *The* ***intention*** *behind the use of "Cost Drivers" and "variability factors" is the same.*
   This conclusion is based on the fact that both concepts – albeit with some difficulty – are interpreted as measures of an activity's output. With this in mind, the difference between them is limited to the fact that the variability factor concept is used generally whereas the Cost-Driver concept is used solely for *products'* utilization of activities.

57. To a great extent, however, the conclusion also depends on the absolute divisibility of employed resources, and, concerning the timing of implementation, of the reversibility period as well. See Supplement 3 for a more detailed account and examples.

Differences

d. *A cost-recording hierarchy is only implicit in the ABC system's physical, non-monetary level.*
   The lack of explicitness is put down to the somewhat imprecise use of "product" in "product costs", since it can alternately be interpreted as product units, individual product types, product groups, or whole product lines.
e. *There is no characterization of costs grouped according to type of production factor in the ABC system.*
   The disadvantage of this is that the absolute and relative divisibility and reversibility of the resources cannot be evaluated, which jeopardize rational consideration of price adjustments.
f. *The simultaneous recording of production factor cost, department and cost objectives is a useful attribute of the ABC system which has been overlooked due to the research methodology employed.*
   A condition for using the so-called inductive method in identifying such a useful attribute is that ABC researchers are able to find firms which use – and realise that they use – a three-dimensional characterization of resource consumption. This has yet to happen.

The *main conclusion* of the comparison of the two systems is that variability accounting's factor input- and cost statistics contain sufficient data to enable ABC's product calculation - whether product unit-, product-, or product group calculation – to be carried out on this basis.

The chapter closes with a *possible reformulation* of the driver concept, such that it can be understood as a complex of variability factors which utilize a number of the firm's activities. The relevant complex of variability factors is argued to be various sales segments, e.g. product-, order-, and customer types. This reformulated ABC system will be a good supplement to variability accounting's policy control of costs by acting as an "orientation map" or "inspiration analysis" for management. This is illustrated in figure 13 and Supplement 3.

# 3. Porter's use of the Concepts Activities, Value Chains, and Cost Drivers

A central element of Michael Porter's theory of Competitive Advantage is the cost analysis. The main aim of this is a *strategic cost analysis* which can reveal the firm's relative cost position vis-à-vis its competitors. Despite the fact that Porter's aim differs in this respect from that of the ABC system, it is still worthwhile comparing the two, since, as important building blocks of the models, they both operate with "Activities" and "Cost Drivers". In this chapter, therefore, we will be examining more closely whether the meaning and use of the concepts are the same, and in particular whether they conflict with or supplement each other.[58]

The primary focus of Porter's cost analysis is the relative position of the Strategic Business Unit (SBU) in the industry in which it competes. The way in which an SBU is defined in relation to any other SBUs in the company is itself a part of the analysis. In the analysis of an SBU – from now on also just called the firm – this is viewed as a unit which carries out a continuous chain of value activities – a Value Chain (see figure 14 below). The elements in the value chain consist of a series of "physically, technologically, and strategically distinct activities"[59] which is a further specification of the generic activities shown in figure 14. It is to these specified activities that the firm's costs are attributed. In principle, the measure of the relative cost position is subse-

58. The Cooper and/or Kaplan sources used here make no reference to Porter. A search of Cooper and/or Kaplan's and Porter's references using the DIALOG literature-searching system (Social Citation Index) during Summer 1991 also failed to come up with any cross-references. However, a search of other authors who had used both Porter and Cooper and/or Kaplan revealed quite a few (19). This would seem to make the present study even more significant.
59. Porter, *Competitive Advantage*, pp. 38-39.

**Figure 14.** The Generic Value Chain.

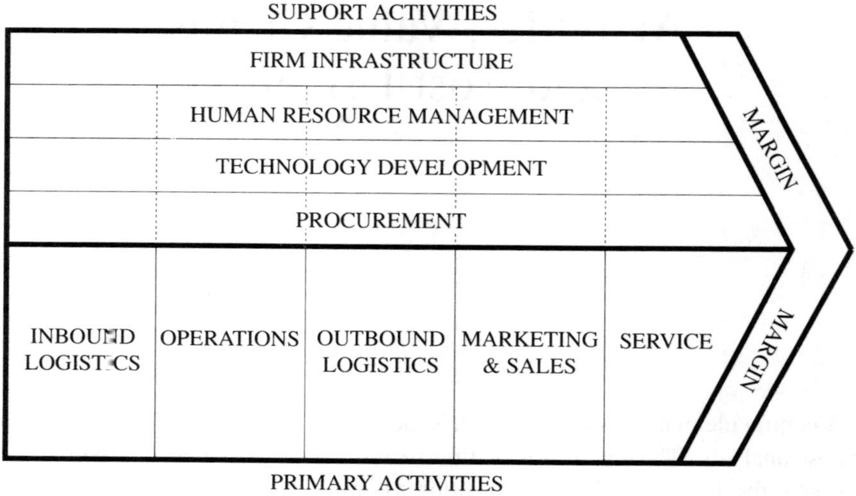


Source: Michael Porter, *Competitive Advantage – Creating and Sustaining, Superior Performance,* 1985, p. 37. Reprinted by permission of The Free Press, A Division of Mcmillan, Inc.; all rights reserved.

quently determined by comparing the costs of the firm's activities with those of its competitors. Comparing activity by activity is both problematic and difficult, however, since competitors rarely – if ever – offer identical products. The abstract solution to this dilemma is a simultaneous analysis and evaluation of whether the higher costs of performing additional and qualitative better activities is rewarded by a higher price for the firm's products and services (differentiation). Porter puts it like this:

> "Value activities are therefore the discrete building blocks of competitive advantage. How each activity is performed combined with its economics will therefore determine whether a firm is high or low cost relative to competitors. How each value activity is performed will also determine its contribution to buyer needs and hence differentiation. Comparing the value chains of competitors exposes differences that determine competitive advantage."[60]

Porter's use of the term "value" reflects the basic truth that ultimately all the firm's activities must be for the benefit of the buyer. The value that the customer attaches to the firm's products and services is measured by the price he is willing to pay. The total "value" which the SBU creates is thus measured

60. Porter, op.cit., pp. 38-39.

by its revenue. Figure 14 shows that the revenues are either used to cover the costs of the firm's activities or go to the "Margin". When at the same time we are told that "Margin can be measured in a variety of ways",[61] then logically, the costs of the firm's activities must also be measurable in a variety of ways – including, for example, at variable, total, or opportunity cost. This is not what Porter means, however. His delimitation of the costing method of activities for use in the strategic analysis shows that it is the *total* costs of performing an activity which must be determined. This can be seen from the fact that all "operating costs" are allocated to the activities which have created the need for them, and that all assets are attributed to the activities which use them. The latter are typically in the form of "capital charges" (interest and depreciations), thereby becoming part of the operating costs. Margin thus means "total net profit", and costs per activity "full cost per activity". The usual cost accounting information cannot be used in this analysis, and the argumentation for this is in complete agreement with Cooper and Kaplan's, inasmuch as Porter states that accounts categories of the type "direct labour", "overheads", and "burden" are not relevant; on the one hand they contain – in the same category – activities with different technologies, and on the other, quite a few costs which belong to disparate activities.[62] At the general level, therefore, there is no difference between Porter's principles of cost attributability for elements in the value chain and the ABC system's principles for creating Activity Cost Pools (ACPs).

The principle for the formation and delimitation of activities is different, however. As described above, Porter's main criterion is that these constitute physically, technologically, and strategically distinct activities. This is elaborated by three supplementary – and partly mutually dependent – criteria: (i) the costs constitute a large or growing proportion of total costs, (ii) the cost structure differs from activity to activity, and/or (iii) competitors perform the activities concerned in different ways.[63] The main criterion in the ABC system, on the other hand, is what could be called "the dissimilarity of the products in their use of the activity". If the products in the firm's product programme do not utilize an activity unequally, then it is not established as such in the ABC system, since it will not result in a difference in the ensuing product costs. The divergency is the result of the difference in focus – while Porter concentrates on the SBU's value chain, Cooper and Kaplan focus on the

61. Porter, op. cit., p. 38.
62. Porter, op. cit., p. 39.
63. Porter, op. cit., p, 45.

segments in this. This difference will be examined in greater detail at the end of the chapter, but first we will take a closer look at Porter's Cost Driver.

Porter uses "Cost Driver" in the following way:

"Cost Drivers are the structural causes of the cost of an activity and can be more or less under a firm's control."[64]

10 such main Cost Drivers – called Structural Cost Drivers in the following – have been identified and employed by Porter:

- Economies or Diseconomies of Scale.
- Learning and Spillovers – learning effects in the single firm versus spillovers in the form of experience effects in the industry as a whole.
- Pattern of Capacity Utilization.
- Linkages – the effect on the size of the costs of carrying out an activity as a function of the way in which the activities in the SBU's value chain are carried out (linkages within the value chain), and as a function of how the interactions between the activities in suppliers' and customers' value chains (vertical linkages) are organised.
- Interrelationships – joint undertaking of activities and utilization of capacity across SBUs within the same company.
- Vertical integration.
- Timing – as regards important cost-affecting decisions.
- Discretionary Policies Independent of Other Drivers.
- Location.
- Institutional Factors.

The above shows quite clearly that Porter uses the concept in an entirely different way than Cooper and Kaplan. To recall the conclusion of the previous chapter, their driver concept (hereafter called "C&K" driver) was perceived as a quantitative – non-monetary - output measure. In the ABC system, this was meant to supplement the usual "volume drivers" with other drivers, with the aim of obtaining an improved product cost figure through a more nuanced attributability of the costs of product-supporting activities to the products. There is, therefore, a world of difference between the two uses of the driver concept. A further indication of the difference is that the ABC system

64. Porter, op. cit., p.70.

only operates with one driver per activity/ACP – as regards attributability to the products – while Porter's strategic cost analysis employs up to 10 types of drivers per activity in explaining the size of an activity's costs. More important than merely pointing out the obvious difference is that *it must be concluded that they supplement each other. Both are necessary in strategic cost analysis, "C&K drivers" to calculate the SBU's product- and product-unit costs, and "Structural Cost Drivers" to explain the difference between these and its competitors'*. Part of Porter's requirement of an analysis of the relative cost position is that the effect of the Structural Cost Drivers must be quantified.[65] Such an analysis is very comprehensive, difficult to carry out, and subject to great uncertainty, since the chances of obtaining precise information about competitors' costs are extremely slim. If such a full-blown analysis is carried out anyway, despite the difficulties and scope, it results in a quantified description of the difference between the firm's and competitors' product- and product-unit costs in the form of a description which is broken down according to the differences in activities employed, and which, for each of these, also describes the relative importance of the respective structural drivers.

Closer inspection of the Structural Cost Drivers used shows that the ABC calculation and the strategic cost analysis deal with depreciation on *unused* capacity in different ways. This is deduced from the fact that one of the possible structural explanatory variables of the difference between the firm's own and competitors' activity costs can be attributed to a divergence in capacity utilization. In the strategic cost analysis, as distinct from the ABC calculation, the costs in question must therefore be implicitly presumed to be allocated to the firm's products and services.

In comparison with the ABC system, "Discretionary Policies Independent of Other Drivers" is of particular interest. Porter gives a number of examples of policies which greatly affect the size of the costs of the respective direct and indirect actions in a lot of the generic activities. These include:

"· Product configuration, performance, and features
· Mix and variety of products offered
· Level of service provided
· Spending rates on marketing and technology development activities
· Delivery time

65. "A firm must attempt to quantify the relationship between cost drivers and the cost of a value activity whenever possible. This will require estimating for each activity the slope of the scale or learning curve, the cost impact of each important policy, the cost advantage or penalty of timing, and so on for each driver." Porter, op. cit., p. 84.

- Buyers served (e.g., small versus large)
- Channels employed (e.g., fewer, more efficient dealers versus many small ones)
- Procedures for scheduling production, maintenance, the sales force and other activities"[66]

As can be seen, it is precisely examples of this type which Cooper and Kaplan focus on. One important feature that these examples have in common is the fact that the cost effects of the policy decisions in question are particularly conspicuous when the SBU's value chain is broken down into sales segments. Porter's analysis of the SBU's value chain includes a possible supplementary study of the cost structure of the various segments the SBU might serve. The reasoning behind the need for such an analysis is the same as Cooper and Kaplan's – amongst other things, the desire to avoid average pricing which can potentially open the door to competitors' profitable competition. To a large extent, the criteria for the determination of relevant segment analyses – e.g. product lines and customer types – also agree, inasmuch as they include, among others, (i) segments in which the value chains used are substantially different, (ii) and where the accounting systems employ questionable allocation bases and methods.[67]

By way of comparison, it can be pointed out that the ABC system - unlike the strategic cost analysis – assumes a predetermined delimitation of the strategic business unit, and focuses on a method for the cost calculation of segments in which the emphasis – in that analysed up to now – lies on product segments. This seems to make the ABC system the calculation procedure which Porter has been searching for (or, in the case of the product segments, assumes) as a replacement for the old full-cost systems. Porter only indicates a few general principles concerning the necessary cost allocations involved. At any rate drivers in Porter's sense – the other 9 - obviously cannot provide a basis or intellectual background for the construction of such an accounting allocation and description.

Only when the ABC system is explicitly enlarged to include other sales segments than product segments can it be said to provide – in all cases – the

66. Porter, op. cit., p. 81. Other examples which Porter cites include: "Process technology chosen, independent of scale, timing, or other drivers", "The specification of raw materials or other purchased inputs used (e.g. raw material quality affects processing yield in semiconductors)", "Wages paid and amenities provided to employees, relative to prevailing norms", and "Other human resource policies including hiring, training, and employee motivation."
67. Porter, op. cit., p. 93.

internal cost information necessary for strategic sales segment analyses. The allocation of costs to segments must continue to be on the basis of "C&K Drivers" or variability factors. Only then can we - in another sense – talk about the individual sales segments as "drivers". It is this fact which, in the previous chapter, justifies our being able to say that the driver concept regained some of its original structural content.

**Summary**

Porter and Cooper/Kaplan mean different things by the concept of Cost Driver. Cooper & Kaplan's Cost Drivers are used to carry out an improved product unit calculation via an activity-derived allocation of the costs of product-supporting activities to the products. Porter uses the concept as a designation for structural variables which explain the cost level per activity unit in each activity of the Strategic Business Unit. Porter thus assumes a calculation which is carried out in the ABC system, but focuses himself on describing 10 structurally different reasons why the firm's unit costs differ from those of its competitors. These two views of the driver concept thus supplement each other in a strategic analysis of cost-induced competitive advantages.

# 4. New Developments: From Activity-Based Costing to Activity-Based Profitability Analysis

Cooper and Kaplan's Activity-Based Costing took a new direction during 1990/91. In this chapter, we describe and analyse these new ideas, keeping the variability accounting system as the point of reference.

Here, the new direction in the continuing development of ABC is taken as ending with Cooper and Kaplan's article in the Harvard Business Review, entitled "Profit Priorities from Activity-Based Costing". Earlier contributions of the same nature are also included in the analysis.[68]

What we here characterize as a new direction, the authors describe merely as a clarification, but, as will be shown, this does not stand up to closer examination. In order to distinguish the two approaches from each other, the new direction is called Activity-Based Profitability Analysis (ABPA).[69] This new development has a number of positive features, not the least being that it meets a great deal of the criticism that was rightly aimed at the original version.

As we saw in chapter 2, the cornerstone of the original ABC version was an improvement of the product calculation through a changed allocation of

68. These include: (i) a speech by Kaplan at the annual meeting of the American Accounting Association in 1989, at which he was also speaking on Cooper's behalf. A paper of the speech is published in Michael A. Robinson (ed.): "Contribution Margin Analysis: No Longer Relevant/Strategic Cost Management: The New Paradigm", *Journal of Management Accounting Research*, Fall 1990, (ii) Cooper: "Cost Classification in Unit-Based and Activity-Based Manufacturing Cost Systems", *Journal of Cost Management*, Fall 1990, and (iii) Cooper and Kaplan: *"Activity-Based Profitability Analysis"*, February, 1990 (draft article).
69. The name originates from the draft article by the authors (Feb. 1990), which says much the same as the article "Profit Priorities from Activity-Based Costing", published in the Harvard Business Review, May/June 1991. "ABP Analysis' is preferred to "ABP Priorities" here, since it better indicates that the method is a form of analysis, as distinct from a decision tool or decision model.

product-indirect costs by means of "volume-unrelated" drivers. These were better at describing the individual products' utilization of the activities which created these product-indirect costs. The original starting point, therefore, was an improved "full cost" *unit* calculation. This is precisely where the new development has taken place, as Cooper and Kaplan now describe the activity-based system in a contribution margin context.

Cooper and Kaplan illustrate these ideas (amongst others) in figure 15 below.

**Figure 15:** Measuring Total Manufacturing Costs.

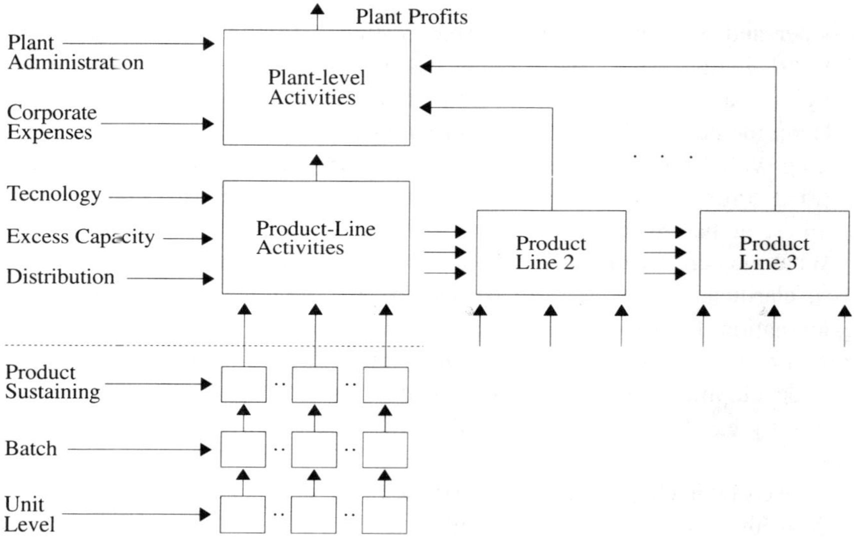


Source: Michael A. Robinson (ed.): "Contribution Margin Analysis: No Longer Relevant/Strategic Cost Management: The New Paradigm", *Journal of Management Accounting Research,* Fall 1990, p. 12. Reprinted by permission of the American Accounting Association; all rights reserved.

The figure shows the authors' ideas of what I shall refer to as a *tiered contribution margin* analysis. The mere introduction of such an analysis marks a considerable break with the previously-described ABC system. It can be seen from the figure that costs are shown at different levels, with the unit level as the most disaggregated object, through batch-level, product-sustaining and product-line activities, to plant-level activities as the most aggregated object, with margin calculations being carried out at each level.

There is a strong resemblance between the previously-described stepped contribution hierarchy and Cooper and Kaplan's general account of the ABP Analysis:

"Figure 1 (here figure 15 and 16) suggests the opportunity of not allocating expenses down from north to south, but aggregating up from south to north. We can compute a unit-level operating margin for individual products by subtracting all unit-level expenses from revenues (price multiplied by production (or sales) volume). From this unit-level margin, subtract batch-related expenses and product-sustaining expenses to compute a product-level margin. Such a product-level margin can be calculated for each product in the product-line. No allocations are required to obtain this product-level margin."[70]

"This perspective adapts the traditional contribution margin approach to the economics of the activity-based analysis. The approach starts by noting that price is a unit-level driver. The more units sold, the more revenue earned. From revenue ...we subtract the expenses of all resources consumed at the unit-level to obtain a figure we can call the unit-level margin for the product. From this unit-level margin, we then subtract all the expenses of resources consumed by the batch and product-sustaining activities for the product to obtain the gross margin earned by the product. The gross margin equals the revenues from sale of the product less all unit-level, batch-level, and product-sustaining expenses. This product gross margin includes all the expenses that can be causally attributed to the individual product. One of the central innovations of activity-based costing lies in its ability to imbed this hierarchy of variability into the reporting of product costs."[71]

"Allocating expenses to individual units sends signals that managers can easily misinterpret. When batch- and product-level costs are divided by the number of units produced, the mistaken impression is that the costs vary with the number of units. But the resources consumed by batch and product-sustaining activities do not vary at the unit level, nor can they be controlled at the unit level."[72]

It can be seen from the above quotations that costs are not allocated/attributed to a given contribution level if they do not vary with decisions about activities at this level. Instead, they are subtracted at the next-higher – and thus more aggregated – contribution level.

However, if we examine the ABP Analysis more closely, we will see that there are *considerable* differences between this and both the stepped contribution margin layout and the variability accounting system's hierarchies in the objectives dimension. In fact, there are also differences between the ABP Analysis in its concrete elaboration and its general description as expressed, for example, in the above quotations. This is discussed in more detail below.

70. Kaplan in Michael A. Robinson, op. cit., p. 7.
71. Cooper & Kaplan, *Activity-Based Profitability Analysis*, pp. 11-12.
72. Cooper & Kaplan, "Profit Priorities from Activity-Based Costing", p. 132.

In figure 16, Cooper and Kaplan give examples of what they call "Expenses" at each level. These groups of expenses are all examples of the aforementioned Activity Cost Pools (ACPs), apart from the "Facility-Sustaining Level", which is an exception (see below). Cooper and Kaplan are not redefining the ACP and Cost Driver concepts here, compared with the original ABC system, merely categorising them.

**Figure 16.** The Hierarchy of Factory Operating Expenses.

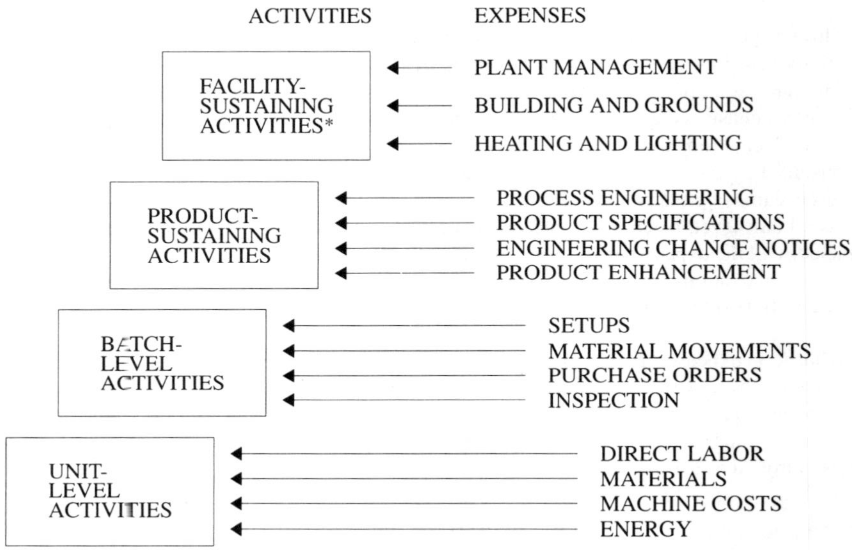


* If plant makes more than one product, this expense is allocated on the basis of value added.

Reprinted by permission of *Harvard Business Review.* An exhibit from "Profit Priorities from Activity-Based Costing" by Robin Cooper and Robert S. Kaplan, May-June, 1991, p. 132, Copyright © 1991 by the President and Fellows of Harvard College; all rights reserved.

The use of the concept "Expenses" in the figure requires a comment. By distinguishing between "expenses" and "costs", Cooper & Kaplan strongly want to emphasize the *availability* of resources (the economic equivalent is expenses) as opposed to the consumption/use (the economic equivalent is costs) of these resources in the firm's activities, and that the availability of more resources than are necessary to carry out certain activities might leave open redistribution or discharge of these unused resources.[73] The present analysis also attaches great importance to such a distinction, but makes it using a more elaborate conceptual framework – e.g. (i) the possibility of resource discharge characterized by the concepts relative/absolute divisibility and reversibility, and (ii) consumption/use through the distinction between the resource input necessary to achieve planned activity output and the actual versus the expected resource input used in actual activity output. The latter distinction enables us to distinguish between efficient and inefficient consumption compared with expected consumption. Without measurement and recording of the actual consumption, we can only distinguish between "standard costs" and "expenses" – which is the foundation on which Cooper & Kaplan's presentation rests in their article – and not an intermediate category of "actual costs". Gradually, as the Activity-Based system is qualified with more and more measurements of actual consumption and use of resources ("direct measurement"), the same categories (which in figure 16 are shown as expense categories) will turn up as cost categories too.

As we saw in chapter 2, the task of the ABC system is, for every ACP, to find a driver which describes the scale of activity and which can therefore form the basis for a calculation of costs per unit of the Cost Driver.

The following account and analysis follows the classification shown above, starting with the most disaggregated level.

## 1. Unit Level

Resource expenses recorded at this level are: direct wages, materials, machine costs, and energy, about which Cooper and Kaplan write:

"...we see the traditional *unit-level drivers* (direct labor, materials, energy and machine-hours) that vary proportionately with the number of units produced. If we produce 10 percent more blue pens, then we will consume 10 percent more direct labor hours, machine hours, materials and energy." (emphasis in the original)[74]

"For unit-level activities, if a firm produces ten percent more units, it will consume ten percent more labor hours, ten percent more machine hours, and ten percent more energy. So,

73. The distinction has been further underlined in an interview with the two authors in which they stress the importance by characterizing it as the latest ABC development, cf. Alfred M. King, "The Current Status of Activity-Based Costing: An interview with Robin Cooper and Robert S. Kaplan". From the point of view of chapter 1 and 1.1 this is surprising.
74. Cooper & Kaplan, *Activity-Based Profitability Analysis*, p. 7.

unit-level costs measure the expenses of resources that are consumed proportionately *with the number of units produced*." (my emphasis)[75]

The term "unit-level drivers" replaces the earlier "volume-related driver", and is a good way of emphasizing that what we are dealing with here is a quantitative factor, with which the consumption/use of the input resources varies with the number of units produced.[76] There is also a positive development from the first to the second quotation, since the driver can be interpreted as being "the number of units of 'blue pens' produced" rather than the resources necessary to produce them. In variability accounting terminology, the "number of units produced" would be described as the variability factor, and the quantity of consumed/used input resources (energy, materials, wage hours, machine hours, etc.), evaluated at cost rates per resource type (excluding machine hours), would appear as production factor costs of producing the product manufacturing objective concerned – in this case, "blue pens". This also results in a greater clarity and stringency in the use of concepts within the AB system – provided the individual activities and accompanying cost drivers are named *separately*: the activity by a concept which directly describes it – e.g. its immediate objective – and the cost driver by its quantitative output measure (load factor units), with which the resources consumed/used in carrying out the activity are expected to vary approximately proportionately.

It must also be noted that, in figure 16, "machine costs" – "machine hours" in an earlier version of this figure[77] – are inserted at the unit level. There is nothing wrong with this as far as the time used on the machines is concerned, but it does not answer the question of how the corresponding valuation is carried out, which is of course the main concern of the economic consideration. On this point, a valuation based on the machines' annual depreciations still seems to be the main one – cf., amongst others, figures 15 and 17 in this

75. Kaplan in Michael A. Robinson, op. cit., p. 6.
76. We assume therefore an approximately linear production function for the individual process steps in the direct manufacturing of individual products and product parts.
77. Kaplan in Robinson, op. cit., p. 8.

chapter – but since Cooper and Kaplan have considered opportunity costs as an alternative, then this possibility must also be assessed.[78]

## 1.1 Machine depreciations at the unit-level

It can be seen from the account of the ABC system that the system operated with an allocation of machine depreciations to product units based on annual depreciations, with a rate per hour based on maximum capacity utilization. At the back of this is the idea that excess capacity does not represent a product cost, but "investment in the future" or "waste".[79] This point of view also corresponds to the one which underlies figure 15, where it can be seen that the costs of excess capacity (non-utilized capacity multiplied by the depreciation rate per hour) are entered at the product-line level. This elicits the following comments (sections 1.1.1 – 1.1.4):

### *1.1.1. Contribution hierarchies: stepped versus tiered*

In the first place, this is a *marked* departure from the above-mentioned *stepped contribution hierarchy*. Using a stepped contribution hierarchy, one is forced – for each classification object (Cooper & Kaplan's product-unit, batch, and product levels, etc.) and each production factor cost – to consider whether the production factor concerned is relatively divisible with the activity, *and* whether the discharge horizon of the production factor is equal to or less than the time period of the classification object. In a stepped contribution hierarchy, both are necessary conditions for entering the cost at the level in the classification concerned. If these conditions are not met, deductions for this cost must be made at a higher level of aggregation. These two criteria are justified by the fact that one can go in at any level of the resulting hierarchy with the interpretation that the contribution margin indicated is the economic figure with which the firm's result will change on elimination of the classification

78. "The resources consumed can be priced (or, costed) by a variety of methods. Early adopters of activity-based systems have used prices derived from the company's historical cost accounting system. In this way the sum of the product cost computed by their new activity-bases system reconcile with the costs computed by their previous, traditional system. But to predict future spending and operating expenses, managers could, as well, use forecasts of future prices *or even resource opportunity costs to price out resource consumption*." (my emphasis) Cooper & Kaplan, *DESIGN OF COST MANAGEMENT SYSTEM - Text, Cases and Readings*, p. 276.
79. See, for example, Cooper & Kaplan, "Measure Cost Right: Make the Right Decisions", pp. 96-103. In Kaplan's case, the idea concerning "waste" can be traced all the way back to Alexander Hamilton Church's publications in the first two decades of the twentieth century, cf. Johnson & Kaplan, *RELEVANCE LOST – The Rise and Fall of Management Accounting*, chapter 3.

object. Neither condition is met, as far as machine depreciations are concerned, when the classification object is the unit level, of course, and when we make the realistic assumption that the economic value of most current production equipment is not diminished through use but as a result of technological obsolescence.

*1.1.2. Alternative cause-and-effect relationships*

It follows from the above that Cooper & Kaplan use another criterion for a cost's attributability to a classification object than that used in the construction of the stepped contribution hierarchy. This criterion – nowhere explicitly expressed – seems to be what could be described as 'a causality cause-and-effect relationship in the physical non-monetary sphere'. For Cooper & Kaplan it is sufficient for the attributability of costs to a classification object that it has been possible, on the temporal/quantitative (non-monetary) level, to ascertain and record the number of machine hours/employee hours used on that object. Thus, in allocating resources to the classification objects, it is irrelevant that they were acquired for the use of several classification objects, either simultaneously or successively, in which case the resource in question is both multifunctional and common to – thus economically indivisible between – these. Therefore, there is no *finality* relationship between classification object and cost. So we cannot speak of a "principle of identity" for the attributability of costs to a classification object, either, since this requires precisely the simultaneous observance of both a causality and a finality principle, cf. Riebel.[80] Since it is precisely the identity principle which underlies the stepped contribution margin hierarchy (further clarified below as the "pure" stepped contribution margin hierarchy), then there is nothing surprising about the two versions being different.

*1.1.3. Inspiration analysis versus decision information*

The form of construction of the ABP Analysis makes it unsuitable for use as direct decision information, which, however, was never the authors' intention.[81] Kaplan uses the term "attention directing"[82] to describe the purpose of this analytical tool.

According to this intention, ABP Analyses are only meant to identify those

80. Riebel, "Die Fragwürdigkeit des Verursachungsprinzips im Rechnungswesen", reprinted in *Einzelkosten- und Deckungsbeitragsrechnung*, pp. 67-79.
81. See, for example, Cooper & Kaplan, "Measure Cost Right Make the Right Decision", p. 103, "Profit Priorities from Activity-Based Costing, pp. 134-35, and Kaplan in Robinson, op. cit., p. 14.
82. Kaplan in Robinson, op. cit., p. 12.

sales segments which show extraordinarily good or extraordinarily poor economic results, enabling the firm's decision-makers to concentrate their energies on areas which are most economically important for the firm. In this sense, the ABP Analysis serves as an *inspiration analysis*. Taken in this way, an allocation of relatively indivisible costs to classification objects can take place, provided that the allocation base corresponds to the classification object's capacity utilization. See Israelsen *et al.*[83] for a thorough analysis of the ABC system as a tool in inspiration analysis, using capacity utilization measures as a basis for the allocation of costs. An example of this type of analysis appears in supplement 3.

Even from the point of view of an inspiration analysis, the allocation of equipment depreciations to classification objects using capacity utilization measures is not without problems. In the first place, there is the problem of determining the economic lifetime of the asset, which has a significant effect on the total amount to be allocated per annum, and secondly, there is the question of the activity level in the allocation base – actual utilization, budgeted utilization, normal utilization, or maximum utilization. Amongst these, maximum utilization is by far the most preferable, in order to avoid activity-derived fluctuations (cf. the discussion in chapter 2.4). But determining maximum utilization is not unproblematical either. Solely as an indication of the problem, it requires knowledge and/or decisions within the following areas: (i) determination of the relevant number of shifts, (ii) the intensity of utilization per orthodox hour, (iii) the degree of harmony in the composition of the available equipment, where the lack of harmony precludes maximum utilization of the individual machine, (iv) batch sizes used (which, incidentally, in itself implies that machine depreciations per machine hour can also occur at the batch level in an ABP or inspiration analysis), (v) machines/machine classes with the same kind of service ability, but with different efficiency (cf. chapters 2.2 and 2.3), and lastly, (vi) equipment maintenance policy and practice. Since the reason for allocating machine depreciations to smaller units of classification than is warranted by the absolute and relative divisibility of machine costs is a tentative requirement that the "contribution segment" must cover the long-term consequences of machine costs, an evaluation of the depreciation amount at "specific replacement cost" would be preferable. However, since the purpose of the analysis is inspiration and not decision information, it would be advantageous to put off the retrieval of information about this until those areas – hopefully few – have been identified in the

83. Israelsen *et al*, "Nye Økonomistyringsudfordringer", pp. 106-20.

provisional analysis (with the use of historical costs), where such information can influence the result of the analysis.

*1.1.4. The level at which excess capacity is placed depends on the structure of the production process*

In conclusion, it should be noted that placing the cost-based economic evaluation of excess capacity on the "product-line" level assumes that machine capacity is used for a specific product line. Such an assumption is not fulfilled in firms with a so-called V-shaped or T-shaped production-flow structure,[84] for example, unless the term "product line" includes the firm's entire range of products. In these types of firms, depreciations for unused capacity in the early process stages must therefore be placed at the "Plant Level" of the ABP Analysis.

## 1.2. Evaluation of Resource Use at Opportunity Cost

The possibility of evaluating resource utilization at opportunity costs is a new departure compared with the original ABC system. As will be shown, however, such an evaluation does not harmonize with either the presented format or the purpose of the ABP Analysis.

It is well-known that opportunity costs are derived from the firm's plans for the future. The basis of the ABP Analysis, on the other hand, is the firm's historical accounting records and other statistical records, and its purpose is to identify areas of activity where increased efforts or changed behaviour are urgently needed. Therefore the results of the ABP Analysis *precede*, and are an input of, the firm's non-routine considerations and its planning and budgetary processes. *Logically*, therefore, the use of opportunity cost evaluation is only possible *after* the ABP Analysis has been carried out. The concluding chapter examines whether it makes sense for certain types of firms to base their external price determination on a combination of ABC calculation and – for selected resources – opportunity cost.

The evaluation of machine utilization at opportunity cost would not harmonize with Cooper & Kaplan's version of the ABP Analysis in figure 15, either. If capacity is not being fully utilized, then the opportunity cost element

84. A V-shaped production flow is characterized by the fact that a relatively small number of input materials is, after several successive process stages, turned into many different finished goods. This is, for example, typical in joint production processes. In T-shaped production, most of the early process stages are common to the whole product line, while the finished goods first become distinguishable in the last stage/stages. See Umble and Srikanth, *Synchronous Manufacturing*, for a more detailed description and discussion of these forms of production.

will be zero at both the unit- and product level, a consequence of the fact that, in this situation, opportunity cost is zero per machine hour. If capacity is scarce, then the whole of the opportunity cost – calculated as maximum (practicable) capacity multiplied by the "largest foregone contribution margin"[85] – goes to the unit level (possibly some to the "batch" level, depending on the planning and recording system used) and nothing to the product-line level, because capacity is not – or should not be – idle.

## 2. Batch Level

The resource inputs needed for carrying out all batch-related tasks are dependent on the number of, and investment of time in these activities, but independent of the number of units in the batch concerned. This applies for the "setups" discussed in chapter 2, of course, but also for a lot of other batch activities. Figure 16 shows some other examples: "number of material movements", "number of purchase orders", and "number of inspections" (the latter possibly specified in the quality test of purchased materials and the first product/products in a production batch).

Special attention should be paid to the fact that, under all normal and realistic circumstances, there is an incongruent number of batches. At least, this applies as far as the size of purchase orders and production orders is concerned ("number of purchase orders" is not the same as "number of setups", of course) – not to mention the number of sales orders, which is not dealt with in a batch perspective in figure 16, since these costs fall outside the framework of "Factory Operating Expenses". The batch problem is therefore more intricate than Cooper & Kaplan's figure would suggest. At this level, we need to operate with a batch activity and accompanying ACP for each incongruent activity, and for each of these to find and record a relevant driver. The identification of drivers at the batch level is therefore more complex than at the unit level, where the number of manufactured units per product/component is sufficient. Thus there are three batch drivers in the following numerical example from Cooper & Kaplan (reproduced here as figure 17), namely "number of setups", "number of production runs", and "number of material moves".

85. Note that the narrow definition of opportunity costs is still being used.

**Figure 17**: ABC Analysis of a Drive Shaft

| | | | |
|---|---|---|---|
| **Unit-Level Expenses** | | | |
| Materials | | $ 7.07 | |
| Direct Labor | | 2.36 | |
| Direct Labor Overhead | @ 111% per DL$ | 2.62 | |
| Machine Hour Overhead | @ $16.71 per MHr | 5.15 | |
| Total per unit | | $17.20 | |
| **Total Unit-Level Expenses for 80 parts @17,20** | | | **$1,376** |
| **Batch-Level Expenses** | | | |
| 2 setups @ 4.2 hours each | @ $33.76/setup hour | $284 | |
| 2 production runs | @ $114.27/run | 228 | |
| 4 material moves | @ $19.42/move | 78 | |
| Total per batch | | $590 | |
| **Total Batch-Level Expenses** | | | **590** |
| **Product-Sustaining Expenses** | | | |
| 1 part | @ $487 | $487 | |
| **Total Product-Sustaining Expenses** | | | **487** |
| **Total Product Expenses** | | | **$2,453** |
| **Facility-Sustaining Expenses** | | | |
| **(allocated to product @ 9.1% of value added)** | | | **172** |
| **Total Expenses Allocated to Product** | | | **$2,625** |



It can be seen from the figure's batch level – agreeing completely with what we stated above concerning depreciations – that the batch drivers are used to calculate the allocation of costs in each of the three ACPs: "setups", "production runs", and "material moves". On the other hand, these are not allocated to the unit level, unlike the ABC system discussed in chapter 2.

The figure also illustrates – and which was already mentioned in chapter 2.3 – that we can be forced to carry out arbitrary allocations of batch costs to the unit level in a number of different sales segment analyses, or, alternatively – as in the stepped contribution hierarchy – to deduct them at such a high level of aggregation that arbitrary allocations are avoided, which implies a higher level of aggregation than is shown in figure 17. This batch problem is avoided only in the case where the illustrated "drive shaft" appears exclusively as a finished product to *one* customer. If, on the other hand, it also figures as a component in other, more processed products, and/or is sold to several customers, then the aforementioned choice arises in a segmented economic analysis of both products and customers.

## 3. Product-Sustaining Level

This level contains the cost evaluations of resources used to sustain and improve the possibility of producing a given product, but which are kept independent of the current scale of production – i.e. independent of the batch and unit levels. Examples can be seen in figure 16: maintenance of the product's bill of materials/-operations, product modification or engineering change notices, as well as process and product improvements. All the resources used in these activities must be identified and recorded per product in order to be assigned at the level shown in figure 15 (and in the example in figure 17). Alternatively – but less accurately – the demand of recording the product-specific use of the input resources can be dropped, letting a driver per type of activity form the basis of allocating costs to products instead (NB: not product units). In this case, the method corresponds to the above-mentioned "indirect measurement".

Cooper & Kaplan's intention in classifying each product's resource consumption/use into three levels is to improve the function of calculations as a decision-support tool compared with the situation where only "unit-level" drivers are used. They put it like this:

> "Once a richer array of drivers of resource consumption is recognized, then many more of an organization's resources can be seen to *vary* with decisions made about products and production processes."[86] (Emphasis in the original)

Or, as stressed by Cooper:

> "ABC systems (called ABP Analyses in the present discussion) identify costs that vary in proportion to changes other than production volume, for example, the number of batches made, or the diversity of products manufactured."[87] (Parenthesis added)

The above conclusion is extremely problematical without the clarifications or modifications which result from the cost evaluation method used: the economic consequences of product- and process decisions for an individual product are not independent of simultaneous decisions for other products in the

86. Cooper & Kaplan, *Activity-Based Profitability Analysis*, p. 9.
87. Cooper, "Cost Classification in Unit-Based and Activity-Based Manufacturing Cost Systems", p. 5.

product line (which is a consequence of ignoring the relative divisibility of the factors of production with the classification object), and the timing of the economic consequence is unspecified (which results from ignoring the discharge horizon of the factors of production – due, in particular, to the inclusion of depreciations). The information is therefore particularly suitable as an input in strategic reassessments of product- and process choice, which also fits in well with the ABP Analysis as an inspiration analysis.

## 4. Product-Line Level

The costs of activities relating to the products – though not to a particular product in the product line – are assigned at this level. According to figure 15, these activities include technology-, process-, and product development, which, though not product-specific, are related to a specific product line.

The same figure also shows distribution costs at this level. However, in many realistic situations, these will not be specific to any single product line. This applies in all cases where several product lines share the same distribution facilities. An allocation of these costs to product lines solely on the basis of 'a causality cause-and-effect relationship in the physical non-monetary sphere' is not possible here, since the distribution facilities are used by a complex of elements in the product lines.

The resulting margin at this level must, according to the authors, be used to evaluate whether a particular product line earns enough to cover its costs "in production and marketing". The conclusion is correct, assuming corresponding modifications such as those mentioned under the "product-sustaining" level.

## 5. Plant Level

The costs of all other activities are placed here. What these costs have in common is that, according to Cooper and Kaplan, they are a prerequisite for the sale and manufacture of products and product lines in the firm, but are independent of the breadth, depth, and scale of production in the product lines. Cooper and Kaplan give a number of examples of this:

> "The building, senior plant management, shared utilities (such as plant and lighting), and general support functions (housekeeping, security, and landscaping).... insurance, property taxes, and utilities... the expenses of plant support staff; the plant manager, and the finance, human resources, security, building maintenance and landscaping departments..."[88]

88. Cooper & Kaplan, *Activity-Based Profitability Analysis*, p. 16.

As the examples show, they constitute a judicious mix of production factor cost-, department-, and objectives dimensions, there being no stringent classification of the various dimensions of consumption in the AB system. This is not surprising, however, seeing that it concerns the uppermost costs in the department and objectives hierarchies, since the Activity-Based system's area of interest is the cost and contribution analysis of sales segments.[89] Compared with this, the aforementioned costs are relatively independent. This also explains why drivers are not discussed at this level. However, it does not alter the fact that these costs also have to be analysed and controlled. This is accomplished in the variability accounting system via the control of cost objectives, supported by a calculation of the cost consumption of the respective objectives and the identification and recording of the explanatory variability factors in cases where relevant.

We can now discern a number of hierarchical contribution formats, employing different stratification and classification principles and serving different informational needs. In light of the above discussion four such can be distinguished.

**I. *Pure*** *decision-informational stepped contribution hierarchies*

In constructing this type of hierarchy, a very strict criterion of objectivity and reliability is applied in attributing a cost to a classification object, with the result that costs are not pushed further down a hierarchy of classification objects than simultaneous observance of the following principles warrants:

- Both economically and quantitatively, the factors of production must be divisible with the classification object in order to be attributable to it. In practice, this rules out the possibility of attributing so-called "direct wages" to the unit level. In fact, material consumption is attributable only if the acquisition of materials can be made in individually-chosen and varying quantities.
- The economic equivalent of production factors are not attributed to shorter sub-periods than those to which they are unique. This means that factors of production (including services) which cannot be acquired for shorter periods than 1 year, 6 months, 3 months, or 1 month, etc., are not attributable to shorter periods than these. One consequence of this is that all forms of depreciation are precluded in this type of contribution hierarchy.

The combined consequence of these two principles is that the cost of a

89. Understood as products, product lines, distribution channels, etc.

production factor is only attributable to a given classification object if (i) the underlying absolute divisibility of the factor is less than or equal to the classification object's resource requirement (and thus relatively divisible with it), and given that (ii) the contractual period of the factor is shorter than or equal to that of the classification object, plus that (iii) the discharge horizon of the factor is shorter than the commencement of the classification object's period.

These principles and their consequences are one way of expressing the demand of simultaneous observance of the cause-and-effect relation in both its the causality and the finality sense, and is therefore identical to Paul Riebel's "identity principle".

In reality, the use of the identity principle results in a blurring of the difference between consumption costs and acquisition costs, in other words, a *de facto abandonment of the cost concept* as an expression of the valuation of factor consumption.

On the other hand, the result of the observance of all these demands on the stepped contribution margin layout is that *at each step, the indicated contribution constitutes direct decision information* regarding the economic consequence – estimated in terms of revenue and acquisition costs – of eliminating the contribution step in question. This is, we should add, on condition that there is no significant interconnection between sales of the various products.

**II.** *Stepped contribution margin hierarchy*

This form of contribution is used by, amongst others, Vagn Madsen – not as a logically-compelling, but as a natural consequence of the variability recordings. This contribution format makes less rigorous demands of objectivity than the "identity principle". The cost consumption concept is used in its pagatorian form, which primarily precludes depreciation and imputed interest.

Based on this line of thought, the decisive principles for the construction of contribution hierarchies are:

- that the quantitative consumption/use must vary approximately proportionately with the scale of activity under the classification object concerned (here meant as the cost objective). From this, it follows that there is no allocation of costs from objectives to sub-objectives.[90]

90. On the other hand, costs of multifunctional factors can well be allocated to different objectives - we saw in chapter 1.1, it must be remembered, that this cost characteristic is related to the *production factor* cost and not the objectives dimension.

– that the firm has established a recording scope and recording depth which enables costs to be assigned to those classification objects with which the contribution hierarchy operates.
– that the *effect* of resource consumption on revenue creation, or the reduction effect on other costs, must be regarded as being confined to the period to which the costs are attributed.

Compared with the pure stepped contribution hierarchy, therefore, the discharge horizons[91] and absolute divisibility of the production factors are ignored here.

The principle of only attributing costs to periods of such a length that they are unique to them (a matter of periodical divisibility) is not applied either, but has the result that investment expenditures on equipment, in the form of depreciations, which exceed these periods are not assigned to smaller classification objects than the whole firm (corresponding to the plant level of the ABP Analysis). A more important reason for this procedure, however, is the greater subjectivity which these costs are subjected to in a procurement-derived cost evaluation.[92]

The above-stated principle about taking into account the effect on revenue creation results in all costs which have the character of investments being removed from the contribution hierarchy's specific classification objects. These costs are subsequently treated in the same way as depreciations on equipment and buildings. An example of this problem appears in the next chapter.

It follows from the above that the stepped contribution margin hierarchy *cannot* produce the same direct decision information as the pure contribution hierarchy. However, if we imagine that the relevant minimum period for the stepped contribution margin layout is 6 months to 1 year, and that, in the budget, it is drawn up a corresponding period prior to this, then the difference is related especially to the human capacities with little absolute divisibility –

91. At least, this applies to Vagn Madsen's use of the stepped contribution hierarchy, since, he states, "whether the various elements of the plan are free or tied cannot be seen from the budget", Madsen, *Budgettering*, p. 31. This means that you cannot tell from the budget description which elements are derived from contractual obligations and which are just planned.

92. In a traditional sense depreciations do not, de facto, play a role in Vagn Madsen's economic information *to management*. This is dropped in favour of an evaluation of whether operating profits (before depreciation) are sufficient to cover the expected and planned average investments necessary to stay in the selected business which result from management's strategic considerations and long-term budgets.

i.e. small specialised groups of personnel. But it is precisely these costs which have very limited discharge possibilities, since changes in activity would have to be very extensive before changes in them were possible.

**III.** *ABP Analysis (tiered contribution analysis)*
The requirement of objectivity is further weakened in this form of analysis. Firstly, as a basis for cost-attributability, the finality concept of the cause-and-effect relationship is dropped completely, while the causality principle – according to which the costs of physically consumed resources and the time consumption of other resources can be attributed to the activities to which they have been, or are expected to be used – is retained.

The cost evaluation principle is no longer pagatorian, either, but a "valuative" cost concept which includes, in particular, depreciations. As far as machine depreciations are concerned, the attributability not only takes the form of apportioning a relative share of the investment expenditures to the period, but also of allocating these to the unit level, based on the causality principle.

In addition, costs are also allocated to more specified classification objects than the recordings support. This includes, for example, the attributability of batch costs to specific products (NB – not product *units*) using drivers, unsupported by measurements. In itself, however, this approach does not lead to changes in the underlying logic of the attributability, but is a question of the accuracy or precision in the resulting contribution calculation.

The consequence of these principles for the ABP Analysis is that it *cannot* serve as decision information, but only as a basis for the identification of economically problematic and productive sales segments, though this mainly applies when the contribution segments of the ABP Analysis are products and product lines. In other segment analyses, we need an inspiration analysis instead.

**IV.** *Inspiration analysis*
With this form of analysis, other allocations of costs than those described above under the ABP Analysis can be carried out. The need for further allocations arises especially when the hierarchical segment analysis concentrates on other segments than products, but it also arises here if a lot of in-house components are used in the production of a variety of finished products.

Inspiration analyses also allow the allocation of costs from superjacent to subjacent objectives, and from these to other adjacent objectives. There are limits to this, however, since the need for *allocation must be justified by incongruent batch sizes in purchasing, production, and sales*. This limits it to an allocation of batch costs in purchasing and production to the unit level. The need for these kinds of allocations arises especially in non-product-oriented segment analyses when the firm has a high degree of complexity in both the sales and production function, meaning that the sales function handles a lot of customers, distribution channels, geographical markets, and order sizes, and the production function a lot of raw materials, components, products, and product lines.

This limitation on the allocation scheme suggests that the expanded allocation procedure neither includes the "product-sustaining" level nor any allocation based on "value-added". The latter is not included because it is arbitrary in every sense, and therefore uninspirational, and the former because the costs often have an effect which goes beyond the relevant (typically 1-year) period of analysis.

It is difficult to say for certain whether this inspiration analysis (illustrated in supplement 3) corresponds to Cooper and Kaplan's ABP Analysis when other sales segments than products are concerned. While Cooper and Kaplan certainly point out the desirability and possibility of such analyses being based on activity-based ideas,[93] they have not presented an example of this kind of analysis in such detail that it allows a more conclusive judgement.

**Summary**

Chapter 4 analyses Cooper & Kaplan's further development of the ABC system in the '90s. The authors now talk of ABC as a general tool for determining management's profitability priorities. The change of emphasis between this and ABC's earlier focus on the calculation of total product unit costs is so great that it has been given a new designation here, namely Activity-Based Profitability Analysis.

In this new system, the interplay between segments of costs and revenues – with the main emphasis still on products – is described in terms of a contribution hierarchy. The hierarchy used differs from the usual contribution hierarchies, however. Four types of contribution hierarchy are identified in this chapter, each with different informational aims and different principles for cost allocation. These are:

I. ***Pure*** *decision-informational stepped contribution hierarchies.*
II. *Stepped contribution margin hierarchy.*
III. *ABP Analysis (tiered contribution analysis).*
IV. *Inspiration analysis.*

93. Cooper & Kaplan, "Profit Priorities from Activity-Based Costing", pp. 133-134

The first-mentioned contains direct economic-decision information, since the indicated contribution per step in the hierarchy is the economic contribution which the firm will lose (earn) by eliminating (adopting) the segment concerned, given *in*dependence between sales in the segments. Method II also aims at giving economic-decision information, but does so less precisely than method I, since it ignores the absolute divisibility and reversibility period of the personnel capacities.

The contribution hierarchies under methods III and IV serve to identify sales segments which are in dire need of alternative – and selective – marketing measures. These methods allow the *allocation* of costs to segments in the hierarchy. The inspiration analysis opens up the possibility for a greater scale of cost allocation than the ABP analysis, which in particular is occasioned by the need to calculate relevant product unit costs for use in profitability analyses which focus on other sales segments than product segments. On the other hand, inspiration analysis rules out allocations of product-sustaining costs and allocations based on "value added".

On account of their informational aim, methods III and IV precede the firm's budgetary- and non-routine considerations, which is why an evaluation of resource consumption at opportunity cost is argued to be irrelevant.

## 4.1. Natural versus Problem-Determined Hierarchies

It would be useful at this point, given the alternative forms of contribution hierarchies outlined in the previous chapter, to clarify the difference between hierarchies used in contribution margin layouts and the cost hierarchies used in variability accounting. In chapter 2.3, this difference was described as a distinction between problem-determined and natural hierarchies. This difference can be underlined by an example. The example is also used to illustrate the informational purpose of the hierarchies, by showing the various ways in which the costs are dealt with.

The starting point of any contribution analysis – whether stepped or tiered – is the purpose of the analysis. Which primary segmentation of revenue we need to look at depends on what this purpose is, e.g. a contribution analysis of products/product lines, customers/customer groups, distribution channels, or order sizes. The level or step to which a given cost is *assignable* is derived from this primary segmentation. As demonstrated previously, the difference between the tiered- and the stepped contribution analysis boils down to a question of the *difference in attributability criteria*. The hierarchies of both types of contribution analysis are problem-determined, however, as opposed to the natural hierarchies of the variability accounting system. The best way of illustrating the difference between these is through an example. Figure 18 presents a chart of accounts for the objectives dimension, the content of which corresponds to a number of the information requirements Cooper and Kaplan's example demands, cf. figure 16.[94]

The figure shows four main *adjacent* hierarchies (the material movements objective, product manufacturing objective, etc.), but apart from this, it should be noted that there are also adjacent objectives in each of the four superjacent objectives. The criterion by which cost objectives are established in the chart of accounts is which tasks the firm wants to budget for and provide follow-up information on, provided that the qualitative and quantitative solutions to the various activities involved in such tasks can be stated in relatively autonomous policies.[95] The fewer the cost objectives, the greater the number of costs which have to be budgeted and recorded at higher-level objectives. If, for example, "product modification (ECN)" is removed, then these costs will have to be recorded and budgeted at the "product- and process development en bloc" level instead. Or, for example, if the "material movements objective" is removed altogether, then the budgeting and recording of these costs must be tacked on to the account for "other objectives en bloc". Consequently, solutions to the budget- and recording tasks will be much more aggregated – so aggregated, in fact, that it can be difficult, if not impossible, to find one variability factor with which the consumption/use of resources for the activities in question varies approximately proportionately.[96]

*It is important to note, however, that, in a recording- and budgeting context, the four objectives hierarchies are adjacent – there is no mutual super-/subjacent relationship between them.* It is only in connection with the contribution layout that the hierarchy between these adjacent hierarchies is established, and this contribution hierarchy – and thus the objectives' position in it – is dependent on the purpose of the analysis.

94. The inspiration for the "material movements objective" is an example in Cooper & Kaplan, "Measure Cost Right: Make the Right Decision", p. 99.

95. That policies can only be formulated *relatively* autonomously is due to the fact that all the firm's policies must naturally be harmonized with each other so as to form a coherent and economically viable whole.

96. However, we must not forget that the recordings simultaneously encompass "type of production factor" and "department". In a budgeting context, this suggests that we can estimate costs based on variability factors for combinations of "type of production factor", "department", and "objective".

**Figure 18**: An objectives hierarchy corresponding to Cooper & Kaplan's example.

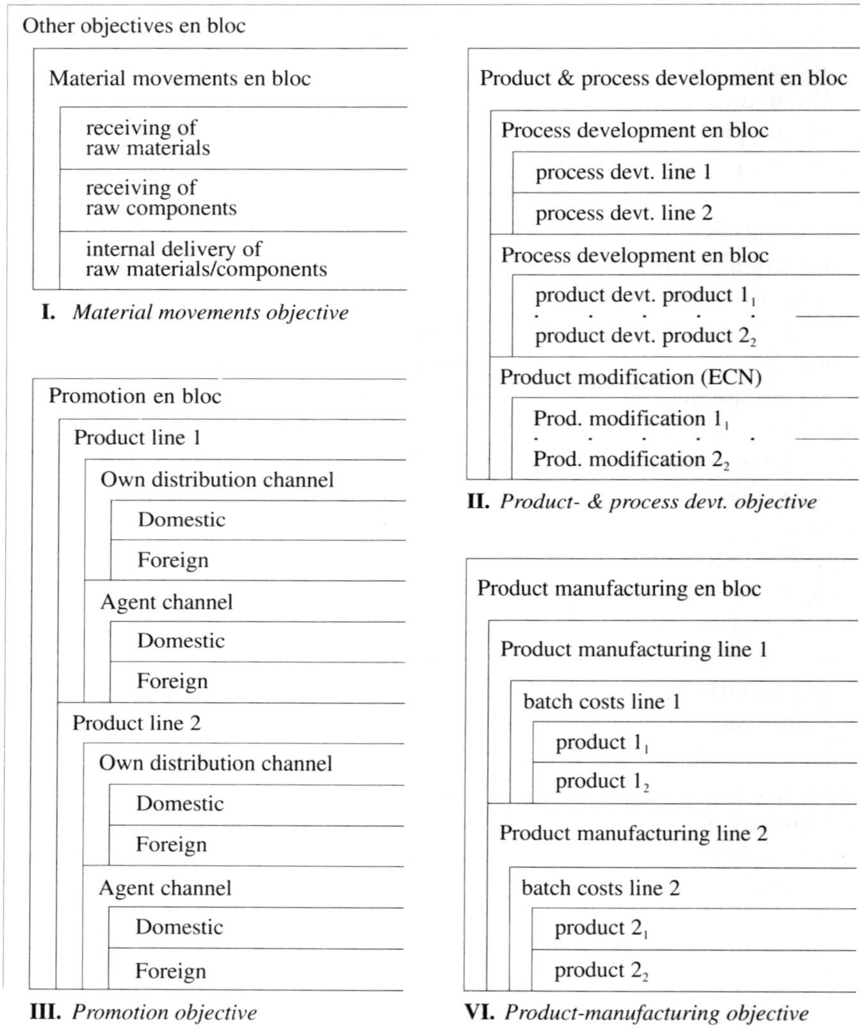


This is illustrated in figures 19 and 20, two contribution hierarchies – with the firm's products and distribution channels respectively as the focus of analysis – which are based on the objectives in figure 18. The degree of specification in the two contribution layouts corresponds to the recording scope of the variability accounting system, which is necessary if registrations against the chart of accounts in figure 18 are to be carried out.

**Figure 19**: Contribution margin analysis of products and product lines.

| Products: | $1_1$ | $1_2$ | $2_1$ | $2_2$ |
|---|---|---|---|---|
| Revenue | – | – | – | – |
| Product-specific product manufacturing | – | – | – | – |
| CM 1 | a | a | a | a |
| Product-specific product modification/(ECN) | – | – | – | – |
| Product-specific product devt. (?)[1] | – | – | – | – |
| CM 2 per product | b | b | b | b |
| Σ CM 2 per product | B | | B | |
| Product-line-specific batch costs | – | | – | |
| Product-line-specific manufacturing costs | – | | – | |
| Product-line-specific process devt. | – | | – | |
| Product-line-specific promotion[2] | – | | – | |
| CM 3 per product line | c | | c | |
| Σ CM 3 per product line | | C | | |
| Product manufacturing en bloc | | – | | |
| Product-/process devt. en bloc | | – | | |
| Promotion en bloc | | – | | |
| Material movements en bloc[3] | | – | | |
| Other objectives en bloc | | – | | |
| Gross profit margin, pre-depreciation | | GPM | | |

**Notes**:
1. The significance of the question mark is explained in the accompanying text.
2. plus all subjacent objectives from figure 18.
3. plus all subjacent objectives in the material movements hierarchy.

A comparison of the two contribution layouts shows that, in several cases, the various cost objectives are placed at different levels. This applies, for example, to all activities connected to products or product lines, inasmuch as they are not unit-dependent. In a distribution channel analysis, these activities' costs can only be deducted at the most aggregated contribution level, since a more disaggregated allocation would result in arbitrariness in the form of *allocation of segment costs*. Even batch costs which are specific to product lines have to

**Figure 20**: Contribution margin analysis of distribution channels.

| | **Own distribution channel** | | **Agent channel** | |
|---|---|---|---|---|
| | Domestic | Foreign | Domestic | Foreign |
| Products | $1_1$ $1_2$ $2_1$ $2_2$ | $1_1$ $1_2$ $2_1$ $2_2$ | $1_1$ $1_2$ $2_1$ $2_2$ | $1_1$ $1_1$ $2_1$ $2_2$ |
| Revenue | – – – – | – – – – | – – – – | – – – – |
| Prod. -specific product manufacturing | – – – – | – – – – | – – – – | – – – – |
| Prod. -specific product modification/(ECN) (?) | – – – – | – – – – | – – – – | – – – – |
| CM I per product per channel per country | x x x x | x x x x | x x x x | x x x x |
| Σ CM I per channel per country | X | X | X | X |
| Segment-specific promotion costs | – | – | – | – |
| CM II per channel per country | y | y | y | y |
| Σ CM II per channel per country | Y | | Y | |
| Channel-specific promotion | – | | – | |
| CM III per channel | z | | z | |
| Σ CM III per channel | Z | | | |
| All other objectives | – | | | |
| Gross profit margin, pre-depreciation | GPM | | | |

**Note**: The significance of the question mark is explained in the accompanying text.

be placed in aggregated form when, as here, the size of production and sales orders is assumed to be incongruent. In the contribution hierarchy for products, on the other hand, there is no problem in placing them at more specific contribution levels. From this, it can also be seen that *it is not always possible to exploit the recording depth of the variability accounts* in all contribution hierarchies, because *the question of what segment costs are is relative to the purpose of the analysis.*

The question marks in both figures indicate some important prerequisites for the assignment of these cost objectives. The one in figure 19 is to show that the costs of "product-specific product development" are only correctly placed to the extent that product development has been applied to products sold during the period. Thus the level at which the costs are assigned is also a function of the length of the period of analysis. The question mark in figure 20 is to show that the costs of "product-specific product modification" are only correctly placed if they are at the same time market- or customer-specific.

The above contribution layouts are both examples of "stepped contribution hierarchies", using the principles outlined under point II in the previous chapter. We can now turn to the difference between this and Cooper & Kaplan's form of analysis.

The ABP Analysis goes considerably further in allocating costs, since they are also attributed to specified contribution levels even in cases where measurements of the quantitative consumption *do not* exist, which is Cooper's "indirect measurements". For example, allocation of batch costs to products (NB – not product *units*), also in cases where recordings have only been carried out per product line – as in figure 18 – or, even less reliably, where the recordings only embrace a specification level which corresponds to "batch costs en bloc". As far as material movement costs are concerned, they too will be allocated to products (NB – still not product *units*) via an allocation per batch, even in cases where the only recordings which exist are those of total material movement costs and total number of batches moved.

All in all, the result of Cooper & Kaplan's approach is that the costs of some cost objectives – other things being equal, i.e. with the same recording depth – can be pushed further up the contribution hierarchy.

However, the most significant difference is that, in an ABP Analysis, machine depreciations are assigned to the unit level – in a corresponding margin analysis, assigned to the most specified contribution level – while those in the stepped contribution layouts shown are not included at all.

Figure 18 is framed in such a way as to illustrate how carefully and accurately natural hierarchies have to be constructed.

One of the figure's adjacent objectives hierarchies consists of a hierarchy of promotion costs (no. III in figure 18). *In fact, this hierarchy is not natural at all, but problem-determined.* The chart of accounts shows only one possible hierarchical structure for the three chosen independent *attributes* in the objectives' characterization, which consists of a *product attribute* (which product/products are promoted), a *distribution-channel attribute* (which channel/channels are used for sales-promoting activities), and a *geographic attribute* (specifying the countries in which the promotion activity takes place).

Using these three attributes of consumption, 6 (=3!) different objectives hierarchies can be constructed. Three such hierarchies are shown in figure 21 below. (The reader can ignore the italicized numbers for the time being – they will be explained later.)

**Figure 21**: Alternative hierarchies for promotional activities.

(A)

- Prom. en bloc *5+8+9*
  - Product line 1 *7*
    - Own dist. channel *4*
      - Domestic *1*
      - Foreign
    - Agent channel
      - Domestic *3*
      - Foreign
  - Product line 2 *6*
    - Own dist. channel
      - Domestic
      - Foreign *2*
    - Agent channel
      - Domestic
      - Foreign

(B)

- Prom. en bloc *4+6+7+9*
  - Own dist. channel *8*
    - Domestic
      - Product line 1 *1*
      - Product line 2
    - Foreign
      - Product line 1
      - Product line 2 *2*
  - Agent channel
    - Domestic *5*
      - Product line 1 *3*
      - Product line 2
    - Foreign
      - Product line 1
      - Product line 2

(C)

- Prom. en bloc *4+5+7+8*
  - Domestic
    - Product line 1
      - Own dist. channel *1*
      - Agent channel *3*
    - Product line 2 *6*
      - Own dist. channel
      - Agent channel
  - Foreign *9*
    - Product line 1
      - Own dist. channel
      - Agent channel
    - Product line 2
      - Own dist. channel *2*
      - Agent channel

Note: The italicized numbers, explained in the accompanying text, are from figure 22.

If the chart of accounts is to have an a priori fixed hierarchy for these costs – which seems to be the case in Vagn Madsen's variability chart of accounts[97]

97. It is not at all easy to determine whether this is in fact so, but, in connection with a shown example, it is based on, amongst others, the following statement:

> "The further assignment of the costs of distribution and sales objectives by region is thus illustrated purely by example, and could conceivably be substituted by all sorts of other groupings which were more relevant to the individual firm, e.g. a

– then a choice will have to be made between these possibilities, with all the priority-derived difficulties which this implies. More important, however, is that, *no matter which hierarchy is chosen, the choice leads to loss of information*. This is what the italicized numbers in figure 21 demonstrate. These numbers illustrate the cost of promotion activities in the various sales segments. The attributes to which the activity is limited are, for the individual cost consumptions, shown in figure 22.

**Figure 22**: Examples of promotion costs with one, two, and three significant attributes.

| Product line | | | Distribution channel | | | Country | | | Costs |
|---|---|---|---|---|---|---|---|---|---|
| Both | Line 1 | Line 2 | Both | Own | Agent | All | Domestic | Foreign | 1m DKK |
| | x | | | x | | | x | | 1 |
| | | x | | x | | | | x | 2 |
| | x | | | | x | | x | | 3 |
| | x | | | x | | x | | | 4 |
| x | | | | | x | | x | | 5 |
| | | x | x | | | | x | | 6 |
| | x | | x | | | x | | | 7 |
| x | | | | x | | x | | | 8 |
| x | | | x | | | | | x | 9 |

The first three cost items in figure 22 are characterized by the fact that all three attributes are required in order to give an adequate characterization of the scope of the promotion activities. The next three require two attributes, and the

classification by product types, if different distribution or sales channels are used for them, a classification by country and city, or customer categories." (Madsen, *Regnskabsvæsenets opgaver og problemer*, p. 139)

This is taken to mean that of course the individual firm can choose, but that *a choice has to be made*. On the other hand, similar attributes to the ones used here crop up as adjacent characteristics of costs of advertising in another example: Madsen, *Bidrag til Belysning af Rationaliseringsproblemerne i Industrivirksomheder*, figure 21, p. 82.

rest only one attribute. If these costs are to be assigned to a set of variability accounts in the cost-objectives hierarchy, then they must be recorded as shown by the italicized numbers in figure 22. A comparison of the recordings in figures 21 and 22 reveals that there is a loss of information in figure 21. This is not true for all the recordings, however, viz. those where all three attributes are required to characterize the consumption, while for all the others, it depends on the chart of accounts chosen. An overview of those cases where information is lost/not lost is shown in figure 23.

**Figure 23**: Listing of the information loss of recordings as a function of the chosen hierarchical chart of accounts.

| Example amount | fig. 21, (A) | fig. 21, (B) | fig. 21, (C) |
|---|---|---|---|
| 1 | no | no | no |
| 2 | no | no | no |
| 3 | no | no | no |
| 4 | no | yes | yes |
| 5 | yes | no | yes |
| 6 | yes[1] | yes | no |
| 7 | no | yes | yes |
| 8 | yes | no | yes |
| 9 | yes | yes | no |

1. The information loss consists solely of the fact that it does not show that the activity is limited to the domestic market.

The problem of dealing with problem-determined hierarchies as though they were natural hierarchies occurs when no distinction is made between the cost-objectives dimension on the one hand, and its attributes on the other. This distinction was introduced in chapter 1.1 precisely to avoid, amongst other things, this sort of problem. There is no hierarchy between the various attributes ("product", "distribution channel", and "country" in the example) of the cost objective (promotion costs in the example). The existence of a hierarchy in the objectives dimension depends on whether the cost in question (identified by several attributes) is fixed (in the relativised sense of fixed and variable costs) vis-à-vis costs recorded against other objectives. If this is the case, then a super-/subjacent relationship – a natural hierarchy – exists between them. If, on the other hand, the cost objectives in question are functionally independent of each other, then they appear as adjacent objectives in the interpretation of variability accounting presented here. If there is any doubt about whether to place the cost objectives as super- or subjacent objectives in a variability chart of accounts, then it would be best to set them up as adjacent objectives in the database of recordings. The super-/subjacent relationship is hereby shifted to a decision in connection with the problem-derived retrieval from the database. This solution is feasible because the determination of the super-/subjacent relationship is *not an empirical but a logical phenomenon.*

**Summary**

By means of an example, the following is demonstrated:

1. Natural and problem-determined hierarchies are different. The former are unchanged with an unchanged recording scale, and are contained in variability accounting's cost recordings, where the objectives hierarchy is determined by both the relativised fixed/variable relationship between the resource consumptions and the desired recording depth. Problem-determined hierarchies, on the other hand, are a function of the changing purposes of the analysis, which thus determines which step the various cost objectives are placed at.
2. The problem-determined placing of the cost objectives in the stepped contribution margin hierarchy – method II in the previous chapter – depends on the length of the analysis period.
3. One cannot utilize the whole of the recording depth of the variability accounting system in every stepped contribution margin hierarchy.
4. The contribution model of the ABP analysis "pushes" costs further up the contribution hierarchy than the recordings support, and further up than the costs' variability would suggest – this last as a result of the placing of depreciations at the unit level.
5. It is important to distinguish between the objectives dimension as such and its descriptive attributes. Failing to do so will very likely result in a loss of information. There is a natural hierarchy of superjacent, subjacent, and adjacent objectives between the cost objectives, not between its descriptive attributes. A possible way around the problem is to eliminate the natural hierarchy in the recording database, since the super-/subjacent relationship between the cost objectives is logical determined, as distinct from one that is determined empirically.

# 5. Activity-Based Costing as a Basis for Calculation and Sales Price Determination – A Reformulation

Up to now, the construction of an activity-based system has been examined and evaluated without regard to the characteristics, or situation, of the firm in which it will ultimately be implemented. The conclusions reached so far are therefore generally valid for all types of firms. The overall conclusion is that, as a basis for external price determination, an unmodified use of Cooper and Kaplan's ABC calculation is problematic, and that an ABC analysis can be an inspirational but not a decision-making basis for a revisal of the firm's sales price policy or its market policies in general.

In this chapter, we return to the question of the firm's external price determination and the role of the ABC calculation in relation to this. As we saw in chapter 2.2, cost description in the ABC system is centred on the product unit, or product. This implies that, as an historic accounting system, the ABC system produces ex post calculations of product/product-unit costs. However, since, as we have seen, these contain a lot of costs which are not "volume-driven", the system systematically produces activity-change-derived differences compared with the firm's ex ante calculations. This obviously occurs at the product-unit level, where the activity-derived variations in the ex post calculation results from an allocation of batch-related and product-sustaining costs to the unit level. But activity-derived differences also appear even when the ex post calculation has been limited to the product or product-group level. These differences can be caused by changed order sizes in sales, production, materials purchases, etc., changes which might not even have anything to do with the product in question. It is important to realise, however, that, on account of the imputed connection with full capacity utilization, attributing machine depreciations to the unit level does not in itself lead to the underlined variations, and that the variation in the calculation will be substantially less than if volume-related (unit-based) drivers had been used exclusively. *But*:

Paradoxically, we do not need this ex post calculation system to achieve what is, or what should be, the more fundamental ambition of the ABC system, namely to enable the firm – through its overall product, marketing, and sales policies (including price policy) – to avoid sales segments which, in the medium-long and long term, cannot cover the costs of the activities necessary to serve them. *This requires at most an ex ante calculation system.* Not all firms have any use for such a system, however.

The aim of this chapter is *to define the type of firm which needs pre-calculated product costs as a basis for day-to-day price determination*, and for these firms, to outline the elements of *an operational calculation system* – and thus an order-channeling system – *which supports a long-term perspective of the firm's short-term price decisions.* Since it will also be seen that this type of firm in particular has only limited and indirect possibilities of gaining insight into competitors' price policies, elements of *a tactical calculation-monitoring system* will also be discussed.

The very fact that the firm's short-term pricing decisions must not undermine its strategic and long-term price policy is considered here to be the main reason for Cooper and Kaplan's rejection of traditional forms of product-cost calculations.

Cooper and Kaplan's criticism of traditional calculation methods falls into two main categories. The first concerns the decades-long conflict between supporters of full-cost and direct-costing methods, where the source of the conflict can be traced back to different perceptions of what could be called 'the relevant time dimension'. It is in this context that the contribution margin calculation is criticized for not ensuring coverage of long-term costs, and the full-cost calculation for possibly leading to the rejection of short-term profitable orders.[98] This conflict will not be resolved by taking sides, the positions are too entrenched for that, but by explicitly taking into account both the type of firm we are talking about and the market and competitive situation which influences and shapes its sales expectations. More about this later.

The other main, though less common, criticism takes a starting point in the resulting cross-subsidizing effects between different products and order types.

98. Arguments of this type appear in Cooper and Kaplan, "How Cost Accounting Distorts Product Costs".

Here, Cooper and Kaplan point out the undercosting of customer-adjusted low-volume orders and the overcosting of high-volume standard products that results from using volume-related allocation bases in firms which produce both types of products and orders.[99] The consequence – *with an identical mark-up percentage* – is that the firm must be expected to accept an increasing proportion of custom-made orders at the expense of standard products, resulting in (especially with continuing expansion) a deterioration in profits. Furthermore, the result will be the same with direct costing and *an identical contribution margin percentage*, unless the different capacity requirements in production and the support functions necessary for carrying out the order are taken into account. The product- and order types and the calculation effects referred to are an important source of inspiration for the tactical calculation-monitoring system, in the form of tender and accept statistics, developed below.

We turn now to defining the kind of firm which would be interested in a continuous ABC-like ex ante calculation. Producers of one-off orders, in which each individual order constitutes a sizable chunk of the firm's total turnover, have no interest in this kind of calculation. In these types of firm, price determination via tendering varies according to the circumstances, and is of such great economic and strategic importance that it will always be a management affair, and not subject to decentralized routinization. Manufacturers of standard products are not likely to show any interest either, because their prices, quality, and accompanying services are already more or less fixed at the moment the product comes onto the market. The information needs connected with monitoring such a firm's strategy are primarily met by setting up a system for gathering information on competitors' prices, quality, and services, and by implementing a standard direct-costing system to check developments in costs. *The relevant type of firm is the low- and high-volume manufacturer of custom-order products*. This is because, simply, the price cannot be determined in advance as the ultimate make-up of the product is not known prior to the inquiry or tender stage. Therefore only a *set of calculation principles* can be derived from the firm's strategic and budgetary considerations as a basis for the tender pricing policy. On the other hand, some degree of administrative and operative calculation principles is essential in this type of firm, since the many individual tenders makes decentralization an unavoidable necessity.

99. This has, however, also been pointed out elsewhere – see, for example, Kilger: *Flexible Plankostenrechnung und Deckungsbeitragsrechnung*, p. 330 (also in the 1st. edition – 1961 – of Kilger's book).

### a. Tactical Calculation-Monitoring Systems – Tender and Accept Statistics

It is much more difficult for this type of firm to monitor competitors' prices than manufacturers of standard products. Price lists and the like simply do not exist. In the following, we argue that internally generated tender and accept statistics, with alternative ways of calculating products and orders, can be an important tool for indirectly revealing competitors' price policies. The idea is the elementary one that every tender – at the tender stage – is filed in the firm's computer, with details of which product or products the tender involves, the number of units, price offered, distribution channel, and any other information (e.g. public/invited tender, quoted delivery time) which the firm considers relevant in a post-mortem of the subsequent acceptance or non-acceptance of the tender. In connection with this, three types of product costing procedures are carried out, all *ex ante* calculations: a full-cost volume-driver-based calculation, a direct-costing calculation, and an ABC calculation. This enables an expected contribution margin and two types of net-profit estimations per tender to be calculated, based on the actual tender price. Later, when the tenders are sorted into two main groups of accepted and non-accepted tenders, the statistics can form the basis of an evaluation of the *market's* – not the individual competitor's – method of calculation. As previously stated, the aim of these tender and accept statistics is to "reveal" competitors' calculation policies. Not to copy them, but to use them as a benchmark for adjusting the firm's own tender policy, as they must originally have been based on long-term economic and strategic considerations.

While at first glance it might seem resource-demanding to compile such statistics, it must be remembered that most of the information concerning the product, customer, etc., is necessary simply in order to administer and submit a tender in the first place. As for the calculations, they can to a large extent be routinized, since the ex ante calculations which underlie the firm's own tender are assumed to be based on a thorough activity analysis. (More about this below.) The cost calculations necessary for the statistics are thus merely alternative forms of data manipulation using data which are necessary anyhow: the ABC calculation results from an expenditure-derived cost evaluation – based on the annual budget – of a number of differentiated drivers; the direct-costing calculation is a subset of the ABC calculation; and the full-cost calculation supplement is constructed via pre-determined surcharges in proportion to the "unit drivers" of the ABC calculation. The calculations can therefore be automated and computerized.

The product description underlying the statistics is, as suggested, the specifically offered product – not a more generic description. This does not entail considerations of information cost either, as this is also the level at which the actual tender is based. On the other hand, any retrieval of information from the statistics which uses the same depth of product description is of no interest, since the firm makes one-off custom-made products only. A relevant subdivision of accepted and non-accepted offers respectively must therefore follow other criteria. A subdivision into the physical product's 'activity constituents' is hypothesized as being more relevant here, partly because it is here that different suppliers can be expected to calculate differently, and partly because these are the only elements in the firm's production that are recurrent, and therefore the only objects for which the firm can change its pricing policy. More explicitly, it is via the tender and accept statistics that it becomes possible to reveal systematic differences between accept/non-accept as a function of the type of activities involved in carrying out the order. If not, the difference can perhaps be revealed with additional subdivisions into customer types, tender form, distribution channel, etc.

### b. Activity-Based Ex Ante Calculation: The Manufacturer of Custom-Made Products in Varying Order Sizes

We turn now to the question of how the firm's own *ex ante* calculation method can be constructed. Here, we keep the idea from both the ABC system, the APB analysis, and the variability accounting system of a thorough activity description – more so than in the traditional full-cost and direct-costing systems. However, it is suggested that the cost evaluation of these activities for purposes of *ex ante* calculations be carried out in a different way. This ties in with a general argumentation already been touched on in chapter 2.2, and which will now be elaborated:

*In any type of firm, no type of expenditure-derived product cost calculation can form the basis for an optimal external price determination.* In a market economy the argument is the other way around. Which is the optimal price and whether or not it is sufficient to have – short- or long-term – economic interest for the firm is calculated and evaluated on the basis of sets of alternative supply prices and accompanying expected sold volumes. Since this also applies to long-term or strategic price determination, it therefore also suggests that an ABC calculation cannot be justified by elevating it to the status of a necessary minimum long-term price. In fact, Cooper and Kaplan must agree with this view, seeing as how they recommend firms with extensive R&D activities in products with short lifetimes to evaluate revenue and costs over the products' life cycles, which they call "life cycle costing".[100] If the firm is to act in an economically rational way, therefore, it must base its decisions on an ex ante capital budgeting, covering the product's or product line's expected lifetime. Included in this is the *simultaneous consideration* of the product's price-/sales expectations (in addition to the other marketing parameters), and their development, production, and marketing costs. The strategic target market and strategic price level are already decided upon at this point. Compared with this, subsequent annual budgeting, specific product costing and budgetary controls are merely strategy implementation tools, but they are also instruments for measuring and evaluating the need for taking possible corrective measures.

The cost calculation method suggested here employs a combination of consumption and opportunity costs, since none of the existing costing procedures suit the purpose of this type of firm. This can be seen by taking a look at the extremes:

#### *b.1. Extreme A: Calculation of Product Costs Solely on the Basis of Consumption Costs, Including Depreciations*

At the one extreme we have the ABC calculation, in which all resource consumption included in the calculation is at the acquisition price of the resources, including machine depreciations. The justification for this approach is that it is a long-term price calculation[101]; according to the approach outlined here, however, such a calculation *does not exist at all*. Long-term reflections come into play in conjunction with investment considerations. It is also already at this stage in the decision process that interconnectedness in sales, both within and in relation to other product lines, must be appraised, just as any learning-curve effects must also be taken into account, with whatever consequences for price strategy over the product's life cycle this may involve. It is also here – or at the latest in connection with budgeting – that capacity requirements in purchasing, production, sales, and distribution are evaluated. Based on the development and development plans of the other product lines, the economic valuation of the resource consumption for already-acquired capacities takes

100. Cooper & Kaplan, "Measure Cost Right: Make the Right Decisions", p. 102.
101. Cooper & Kaplan, "How Cost Accounting Distorts Product Costs", p. 27.

place at opportunity costs[102], and for others in the form of investment-derived expenditures and payments. There is no room for all these complex considerations in either the ABC's product-unit calculation or in an ABP-inspired single-period product- or product-line calculation. This agrees with what was pointed out in chapter 4 – namely, that neither ABC nor ABP analysis can constitute decision information.

### *b.2. Extreme B: Calculation of Product Costs Solely on the Basis of Opportunity Costs*

At the other extreme, evaluation of resource consumption takes place at opportunity costs. From this point of view, all resource consumptions which cannot be eliminated within the plan period are evaluated independently of their acquisition cost and solely as a function of their contributory effect during the period. This results in a zero value for non-scarce, or "free", resources, and a contribution-derived, marginal-determined positive value for scarce resources.[103] If we go beyond simple examples, in which, for purposes of illustration, we operate with only one scarce resource, we end up in practice with the involvement of Linear Programming (LP). In the type of firm focused on here, however, such a tool will be difficult to use. There are several reasons for this:

- At the point of optimization, neither the physical shape of the tendered products nor their precise content of materials and materials costs is known. Although this does not in itself preclude the use of LP, it does make it more difficult, since the model's criteria function will have to operate with "synthetic products", i.e. product categories in which the category definition follows the criterion of equal contribution margin per sales DKK. One should also be aware of the fact that further sub-categorization will be needed in the many cases where capacity utilization – whether in the form of utilized capacity types or scale of utilization per capacity type – varies.

102. For resources which are unique or devoted to the product line concerned, opportunity costs are zero, since any identified scarcity – rather than a positive opportunity cost – will result in investment-derived expenditures/payments in connection with an expansion of capacity. For resources which are shared between several product lines, the opportunity cost can assume a positive value. This applies especially to capacities which can only be purchased in large minimum quantities and which therefore have a low absolute divisibility.

103. Resources which can be purchased and resources which are dischargeable – can be disposed of – within the plan period are evaluated at consumption cost. Of course, these resources are not scarce in any absolute or relative sense. If the aforementioned wider definition of opportunity costs (cf. chapter 2.4.1, footnote 44) is used, we can say that, here, all resource consumptions are evaluated at opportunity cost.

- The criteria function will be further complicated by a subdivision into order sizes, as the contribution margin ratio, and with it the sales price, in this type of firm must be expected to vary significantly with this. Even though this should be solvable by a surcharge (a cost as well as a price surcharge) on a basic price – actually a basic contribution margin per synthetic product – it only shifts the complexity onto the problem of having to show a linear correlation between turnover per synthetic product and the surcharges concerned.

The main problem with the LP optimization, however, is that it does not make any significant contribution to solving the firm's primary problem, since:

- The *external sales prices are an input, and not an output*, of the optimization. There is, however, a remote possibility of modelling alternative price-/volume combinations and letting the choice between them form part of the optimization procedure, thus making the optimal price part of the output.[104] In practice, however, this method must be abandoned, or reduced to a few partial alternatives.
- Interconnectedness in sales is extremely difficult to describe in the model. Modelling a sales dependency among products must take the form of a linear description or via specified upper and lower bounds on sales per product – in this case, synthetic product. In this connection, the just-as-important problem of interconnectedness of sales between periods – what was previously characterized as a consideration of the fact that 'the firm's short-term price decisions take place in a long-term perspective' – precedes and consequently lies outside the scope of the model.
- The possibility of incorporating forecast uncertainty into the LP model – a significant problem for the type of firm discussed here – is restricted to stating the limits (ceteris paribus per variable) within which the optimal solution applies. Apart from this there are only sensitivity analyses, which can be carried out on the basis of several optimizations with different input variables.

Last, but not least:

- In general, the data requirements of the LP model are greater than the firm

104. The essence of this approach can be explained by the fact that the model, through a determination of the total *extra* contribution of a reduced price (compared with the highest-formulated tender prices) per *extra* capacity utilization (compared with the smallest capacity utilization, corresponding to the highest-formulated tender prices), is sufficient for the reduced prices to form part of the optimal solution.

can provide at the budgeting stage, but fortunately also greater than necessary for the firm to make its tactical decisions concerning capacity availability and product-costing principles.

### *b.3. Calculation of Product Costs Using Consumption and Opportunity Costs as a Function of Uncertainty, Absolute Divisibility of Production Factors, and Interconnectedness in Sales*

Based on the above extremes, an intermediate type of solution can be outlined which is more in keeping with the firm's needs and possibilities. The starting point here is in an assessment of the uncertainty which the firm's forecasts and plans must always be subject to, together with the necessary and sufficient depth of specification of these, so that they can serve as a basis for the firm's necessary tactical periodic decisions.

For the firm referred to, it is considered unrealistic to forecast the volume of sales and production per product and order category prior to the budget period. On the other hand, it is considered possible to decide an *order of priority* between order- and product types within the respective product lines, *and* to budget a total contribution margin (or rather, a profit margin, see below) per product line for the period. How individual specific products and orders will contribute to the total budgeted earnings of the product line is transferred to decision-making *in* the period via the submitted tenders, though these decisions are circumscribed by the limits of the strategic price range. Notwithstanding, to be of any use in making capacity-availability decisions, the firm's forecasting and planning basis must be so detailed that qualified decisions can be made about the size of the firm's capacities in the various functional areas, with particular attention being paid to that part of it which can be periodically adjusted. Here, uncertainty becomes a dominating factor. The uncertainty is primarily related to the forecast of the development in the number of load factor units, and secondly with their conversion to capacity utilization units as a basis for assessing capacity needs. Such forecasts are – although uncertain – necessary in order to make the above-mentioned periodic tactical decisions about capacity adjustments. *The uncertainty of the forecast and the absolute divisibility of the capacities is regarded here as being extremely important for the product-/order costs calculation concerning the use of resources.*

#### *b.3.1. Product-cost calculation of capacities with higher absolute divisibility than the uncertainty attached to their forecasted utilization*

If, for example, there is a *10%* forecast uncertainty, and if the type of capacity consists of *10 or more similar (mutually substitutable) capacity units*, then this capacity, and with it the type of activity, enters into the *ex ante* product-cost calculation at *consumption costs*. There are two main reasons for this choice. Firstly, errors are limited in the case of continued expansion, compared with an evaluation at opportunity costs. This is an important argument in this type of firm, since one avoids unconsciously – via calculation policy – steering the firm into sales segments which, in the longer term, cannot cover the derived extra costs of serving them. Secondly, an opportunity cost evaluation is likely to fluctuate according to whether the capacity is expected to be fully utilized during the plan period or not. It must be recognized that, in spite of the uncertainty, a firm usually decides on a particular capacity size in connection with the adoption of the budget, but, precisely because of this uncertainty, the firm does not know the full extent to which this capacity will be utilized. In this situation, therefore, opportunity cost is, in reality, indeterminate, so any comparison with it will remain de facto abstract.

In practice, this approach is hardly likely to be problematical for direct costing supporters (and not at all for full cost advocates, of course), inasmuch as it corresponds to the usual approach used in dealing with so-called "direct labour" in production. The method merely has to be expanded to include all purchasing, production, and sales-support functions. However, the difference between this approach and direct costing becomes more pronounced when, as here, it is suggested using the same principle on investments in equipment, which has a particular impact on the product-costing procedures for utilization of smaller machine assets. The argument for this is the same as the one above concerning the potentially unconscious economic consequences of continued expansion. The problem with the approach is connected to the fact that depreciations[105] now appear in the ex ante calculated product costs, thus increasing both their subjectivity and the risk of potential short-term decision failures. On the other hand, the risk of an unintentional shift of product- and order types towards unprofitable segments is judged to be greater. Another advantage of the suggested approach is that forecast and planning efforts can subsequently be concentrated on the capacities involved in taking and filling orders during the period, with a smaller absolute divisibility than uncertainty, and with a focus here on the most important capacities as regards costs.

#### *b.3.2. Product-cost calculation of capacities with less absolute divisibility than the uncertainty attached to their forecasted utilization*

Capacities with less absolute divisibility than uncertainty in the forecast can,

105. The hourly rate is conceived as corresponding to maximum capacity utilization, as used by Cooper and Kaplan.

in principle, show up in three different ways: (i) expected maximum capacity utilization does not exceed the maximum capacity available, (ii) though the average expected capacity utilization does not exceed the capacity, maximum expectations do, and (iii) minimum expected utilization exceeds the supply of capacity.

In situation (i), there is no problem in deciding that capacity utilization figures in the ex ante calculation should show up at zero opportunity cost. But what about situation (ii), where maximum utilization *can* exceed available capacity? In the case of these types of capacity, 'contingency plans' are needed in the event that additional capacity is required. These 'contingency plans' contain policies and plans for acquiring additional capacity in the form of overtime, intensity adjustments, subcontracting, etc. This type of capacity also figures in the calculation at zero opportunity cost. The extra cost of the greater capacity utilization must then be expected to be covered via the bigger profit margin, where by "bigger" is meant bigger than budgeted in the average expectations laid down in the plan and the accompanying budget.

In situation (iii), capacity is scarce in all cases. If, as is the case here, there is known to be an absolute scarcity already at the time of determining and implementing the single-period plan, then the failure to plan for expansion must derive from the economic considerations and consequences of the strategic plan. For this type of capacity, it is tempting to conclude – based on rudimentary managerial-economics – that the ex ante calculation of capacity utilization must take place at opportunity costs, which are greater than zero. That this is not accepted without further proof is due to the fact that, so far, no allowance has been made for any dependency between sales orders. Take as an example the potential sales dependency between low- and high-volume orders. The price policy must be worked out accordingly. If this kind of dependency does exist – which can, for example, be the case where the product is part of the customer's prototype production – then it might be considered almost "giving away" the low-volume orders, though such a policy will have to be limited to situations where it is possible to establish an economic connection between the small order in question and the subsequent potential high-volume order. If, on the other hand, there is no sales connection, then we find ourselves in the opposite situation, where the obvious course to follow would be a high profit-margin policy. Here, the size of the profit margin is limited by the competitive situation in the industry and the strength of the "barriers to entry". From this it can be seen that any one-to-one relation or unconditionally invariable relationship between sales price and costs can be ruled out in profit-margin policy.[106] This naturally presumes that the potential sales dependencies mentioned have been analysed and assessed at the strategic level, thus allowing the outlines of the price policy to be laid down from this level. The consequence for the cost estimation of the absolute scarce capacity will therefore differ according to whether there is any interconnectedness in sales or not. If there is no significant dependency, then the calculation is carried out at opportunity costs (based on the plan's average expectation of capacity utilization), otherwise at zero. Though in both cases it is important to note that, through *decentralized* tender-price decisions *during* the period, the goal – within the strategic framework – is to channel the budgeted profit margin towards the product line.[107] It is not hard to work out the average expected profit margin per revenue unit on the above-mentioned basis, but it is precisely just an average: it is not inviolable at the level of individual orders or individual products in the product line. Here, there must be room for tactical market considerations, exercised at the point of tender submission.

The required content of an *ex ante* calculation system which supports the calculation approach outlined above can be summarized as follows:

The ex ante calculation system contains a physical/quantitative – non-monetary – part and a monetary part. In the former, a product parts list is drawn up, together with a description of the activities – adapted to the aggregation level of the monetary calculation system – which the potential product/order directly *and* indirectly gives rise to. The monetary part contains calculation rates for the parts in the parts list and the direct and indirect activities. By calculation rates is meant, for the raw materials in the parts list, the expected purchase prices (if specific purchase prices are negotiated in connection with the potential order, then these), for in-house components, the budgeted direct costs (the respective component objectives) of these, and for all other support activities – i.e. product-manufacturing-indirect objectives – budgeted costs per variability factor unit. The cost valuation procedure of the

106. The case of sales dependency between low- and high-volume orders simultaneously illustrates the necessity of a customer-oriented rather than an order-oriented ex post analysis. Assume, for example, that the mentioned economic connection between low- and high-volume orders takes the form of a 100% refund of the price of the low-volume order if a "high-volume order" is submitted later. In such a case, an order-oriented profit analysis would be worthless.

107. The budgeted total profits on the product line, which is to be covered via mark-ups on individual orders, is different in the two situations. In the case of a positive opportunity cost rate, the total profit is less, corresponding to the rate multiplied by available capacity.

component objectives and the support activities in purchasing, production, and sales is at budgeted *consumption* costs (*incl. depreciations*), *if* the factors of production of these activities have a higher absolute divisibility than the uncertainty in the scale of activity, otherwise at opportunity cost – unless there is considerable sales dependency between the potential orders, in which case they are calculated at zero. The decision about the mark-ups on the respective potential orders is decentralized to the firm's sales organisation, but controlled here by a strategically-set price level and a budgeted total profit figure for the product line in the specific budget period.

The major difference between the set-up of the operative economic product costing outlined here and that of the ABC system is that, in the ABC system, calculations make use of driver surcharges evaluated at consumption costs (incl. depreciations) independent of the absolute divisibility of the production factors – and thus of the actual possibility of capacity adjustment – and independent of the expected demand. On the whole, both the market and the firm's competitive situation occupy a very poor – or at any rate very implicit – position in the ABC system. In its defence, supporters of the system could point out that it is not so inflexible that every order has to be calculated with an equal profit. But while this is obviously true, it must also be pointed out that there is nothing in the system to indicate in which direction and to what extent the surcharges can and must be changed.

A favourable side-effect of using the above-outlined ex ante calculation system is that *it solves the logical flaw* which is inherent in every form of periodic full-cost allocation method used as a basis for external price setting: The allocation assumes an expected scale of activity, and that scale is (partly) determined by the very aim of the allocation, namely price determination.

There are two features in the calculation procedure outlined here which help *eliminate this logical flaw*. The first is that reflections of the interplay between total costs and price determination are incorporated in a simultaneous consideration at the strategic level and at the time of the product line's development and introduction onto the market. Such a consideration must take place in association with a multi-period investment calculation, in this case "life cycle costing". In such a calculation, product-unit or order-unit costs do not constitute decision information, though they can be calculated, of course. The decision information is incorporated in the capital budgeting result and the assessment of uncertainties associated with it. The decisions resulting from the strategic appraisal are commitments to a certain size of basic capacities and a strategic price level.

The second feature is that the period-specific price determination is influenced by market and competitive conditions in the near future (the budget period), and possibly also supplemented by experiences acquired via the aforementioned tender and accept statistics. The operational calculation rates are influenced by and derived from the specific market forecasts and the assessed uncertainties. Differentiation of the mark-ups is limited by the strategic price level, enabling the ex ante calculation system to support the firm's strategy.

In closing, it must be emphasized that the ex ante calculation procedure also enables *the firm's historical cost accounts and their processing against ex post product costing tasks to stop with a basic recording system such as the variability accounting system.* This allows interest to concentrate on comparing actual versus expected activity per cost objective, actual versus expected consumption cost per variability factor, and on ways and means of improving them.

It is regarded as important to stop an ex post calculation of product costs at the level where the *individual elements* of the order and product are identified, partly because individual orders are rarely repeated, and partly because the ex post calculation per order will contain a lot of incidental 'noise' as a result of variations in resource consumption from production run to production run. *The most important reason, however, is to avoid strategic misinformation from the accounting system.* As Cooper and Kaplan have pointed out, an appreciable problem with traditional accounting systems – which in their case means full cost with traditional unit-based allocation bases and a contribution margin calculation based on direct costing – is that, far from supporting, they are often directly at variance with strategically-determined sales prices. Since Cooper and Kaplan's (original) ABC calculation has also been rejected here, and substituted by a calculation procedure which is not solely based on consumption costs – while at the same time maintaining that the resource consumption in the ex post accounts is still to be valuated at consumption costs – *it follows logically that we must completely abandon all thoughts of such an order-/product-unit-centred ex post calculation.* In this connection, it should be remembered that, throughout the presentation given here, historical cost records are still used as a source for inspiration analyses – possibly in the guise of ABP analyses – but these analyses do not include the *individual* orders or products as the focus of their investigation.

**Summary**

As a result of the new direction within ABC, towards what in chapter 4 was called Activity-Based Profitability Analysis, interest in the firm's product- and product-unit calculation as a basis for external price determination has dissipated – or been given a much lower priority – though the problem has yet to be solved using ABC. Chapter 5 addresses this and suggests methods for solving the calculation- and price-determination problem.

The chapter shows how the original ABC reasoning can be turned to good account in a tactical calculation-monitoring system for firms which make custom-made products in varying order sizes, where the sales order is the basis for the calculation, and where the focus is on ex ante calculations. This is done by compiling computer-based *tender and accept statistics* which, using *ex ante data* for all submitted offers, calculates one contribution- and two profit margins based on *direct costing*, *ABC*, and *traditional full costing* respectively. Sorting offers according to the activities involved and into accepted/rejected can, using each of the three calculation forms successively, *indirectly* reveal competitors' (the market's) price-determination methods. These methods can only be revealed indirectly because (credible) price lists simply do not exist in the markets concerned.

The principles of an operational calculation method which allows an economically rational order intake control are developed for use in the firm's own day-to-day price determination. This ensures that the firm's decentralized tender-price decisions have a long-term perspective. The method builds on a combination of evaluation at consumption- and opportunity costs. Calculating the costs at consumption- or opportunity cost is a function of (i) uncertainty surrounding the estimation of the budgeted utilization of underlying capacities, (ii) the absolute divisibility of these capacities, and (iii) whether there is an interdependency between the sale of the various products and orders.

Both the tender and accept statistics and the above-mentioned operational calculation method are based solely on ex ante data. These data are subject to continuous updating via knowledge gained from studies of ex post data, using variability accounting's basic volume- and monetary recordings. On the other hand, it is both inappropriate and hazardous to carry out an order-/product-*unit*-centred ex post calculation using consumption cost data, since it will often result in strategic misrepresentations.

Appendix A

# An Example of the Basic Structure of the Variability Accounting System[1]

The following example concentrates solely on production processes and production departments of a fictitious company, VAMA Inc.. The company's production departments and the organizational structure are shown in figure A1.

**Figure A1**: Organisation Chart in VAMA's Production Area

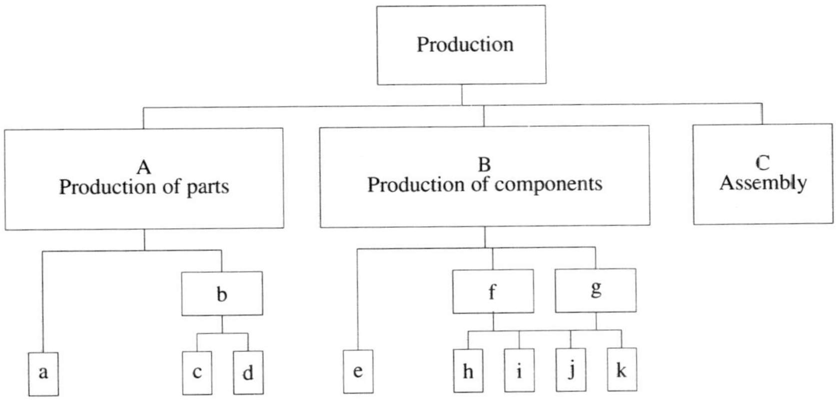


1. Based on an exercise developed at the Department of Accounting, The Aarhus School of Business.

Within production department A, the subdivision into production units is based on the type of material processed, as opposed to department B, in which it is based on the production processes.

VAMA produces two finished products, R and Q. The production flow is as follows:

The following parts are produced in unit "a": X1, X2, X3, X4 and X5. Parts Y1 and Y4 are produced in unit "c", where, in addition, X3 and X4 – together with a raw material, M251 – are used in the production of Y3. Y2 parts are produced in unit "d".

In unit "e", X2, Y1 and Y2 are used to produce part Z1; Z1 is further processed in unit "i", and again in unit "k". In addition, unit "e" is engaged in the further processing of Y3.

Unit "h" receives Y2 parts from unit "d", Y3 parts from unit "e", and Y4 parts from unit "c". The processing of these parts produces output Z2. Z2 is further processed in unit "j".

In the assembly department (C), X1 and Z1 parts are assembled into finished product R. The other finished product, Q, is produced by mounting X5 on Z2.

A summary of the production flow is shown in figure A2.

**Figure A2**: Production Flow in VAMA Inc.

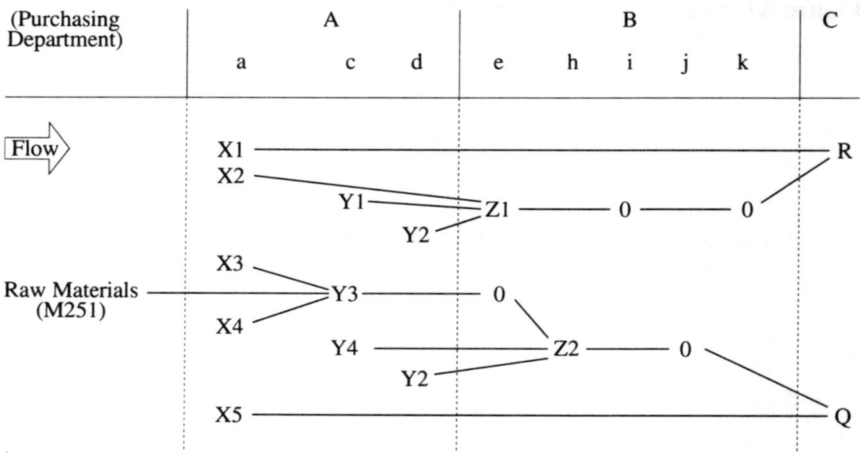


Note: An "0" indicates that further processing takes place in the specified production unit.

To make the registration of costs easier, we assign numbers to the three dimensions of our cost description. See figures A3-A5.

**Figure A3**: Departmental Account Code, VAMA

| | | | | | Code |
|---|---|---|---|---|---|
| Company as a whole | | | | | 7 |
| | Production department as a whole | | | | 74 |
| | | A Production of parts department | | | 741 |
| | | | a | | 7411 |
| | | | b | | 7412 |
| | | | | c | 74121 |
| | | | | d | 74122 |
| | | B Production of components department | | | 742 |
| | | | e | | 7421 |
| | | | f | | 7422 |
| | | | | h | 74221 |
| | | | | i | 74222 |
| | | | g | | 7423 |
| | | | | j | 74231 |
| | | | | k | 74232 |
| | | C Assembly department | | | 743 |

**Figure A4**: Account Code of the Objectives for the Use of Resources, VAMA

| | | | | | | Code |
|---|---|---|---|---|---|---|
| Product-manufacturing objective in general | | | | | | 83 |
| | Y2 | | | | | 831 |
| | | Finished product R | | | | 8311 |
| | | | X1 | | | 83111 |
| | | | Z1 | | | 83112 |
| | | | | X2 | | 831121 |
| | | | | Y1 | | 831122 |
| | | Finished product Q | | | | 8312 |
| | | | X5 | | | 83121 |
| | | | Z2 | | | 83122 |
| | | | | Y4 | | 831221 |
| | | | | Y3 | | 831222 |
| | | | | | X3 | 8312221 |
| | | | | | X4 | 8312222 |

**Figure A5**: Account Code of the Type of Production Factor, VAMA

| | |
|---|---|
| 60 | Consumption of inventory materials |
| 605 | e.g. M251 |
| 61 | Consumption of non-inventory materials |
| 62 | Wages and other costs of blue-collar workers |
| 63 | Salaries and other costs of white-collar workers |
| 64 | External services |
| 65 | Cost reductions |

Note: The two-digit headings are taken from Vagn Madsen, *Budgettering*, Copenhagen, 1970.

Note the coding of costs used in the production of Y2 parts in figure A4. From the production flow shown in figure 2, we can see that this part is used in both Z1 and Z2 – a so-called multi-functional part – and subsequently in both finished products. Our measurement and coding of costs take place *at the time of consumption*, and at the time of producing Y2 parts we do not know how many will be used in Z1 and Z2 parts respectively, so it would be impossible to place Y2 as a sub-level of Z1 and Z2 without introducing arbitrary allocation. In the accompanying production statistics – in chapter 1 called "the firm's factor-input statistics" – we can record the number of Y2 parts used in the production of Z1 and Z2 respectively, in order, for example, to find out if there is a higher percentage of spoilage of Y2 parts in the production of Z1 than in that of Z2.

Observe further that the raw material shown in figure A2 has no separate coding in the account code for objectives. All the different parts that VAMA produces consume raw materials, of course. The kind of material used in the different product parts will be recorded through the dimension of the total account code, called "type of production factor". In this case, the specific raw material, type M251, is coded as "605", cf. figure A5.

The account codes shown in figures A3 and A4 can be significantly simplified in practice. The basis for the account codes shown is the "General Account Code for Variability Accounting" (see Supplement 1), together with the principle of adding one extra digit for every extra sub-level. Let us just imagine here that the code created for VAMA is the one used by the computer.

To avoid possible confusion, it should be made clear that we do not keep three separate cost files for the three different dimensions in our cost description. In principle our total account code has the following form:

| type of production factor code | departmental account code | account code for objectives |
|---|---|---|
| X X X X | Y Y Y Y Y Y Y | Z Z Z Z Z Z Z |

For instance, the cost of raw material M251 consumed in the production of Y3 in department "c" will be coded as 60574121831222, in the type of record shown in figure 2, chapter 1. This way of coding ensures that we keep track of the links between our three dimensions of description. Furthermore, it implies that, in our code for objectives, we do not need separate accounts when only further processing is involved, because this feature is captured by the departmental account code. For example, the code for Z1 – 83112 – is used in unit "e", "i" and "k", but with three different departmental code numbers.

As described in chapter 1, the detail of the account structure depends on both the cost and benefit of information. For instance, in VAMA we could create a more detailed structure in the "objectives for the use of resources" hierarchy by introducing separate accounts describing the "setup costs" of each or some of the parts, components and finished products that VAMA produces. With the account code shown in figure A4, these setup costs will be recorded against "product manufacturing objective in general", but by introducing an immediately superjacent account to some or all of the described product objectives, they could be traced to the number of batches of each part, component and finished product. The most aggregated solution would be to create only one account for setup costs as an immediately subjacent account to "product-manufacturing objective in general". For more on this subject see chapter 2.2 in the main body of the text.

An example of cost objectives outside the product-manufacturing objective is given in chapter 4.1.

## Appendix B

# Numerical Example

**Table 1**: Registration of the number of setups, setup hours, and setup costs per product per machine class for period X.

| MACHINE CLASS | PRODUCTS | NO. OF SETUPS | NO. OF SETUP HOURS | TOTAL DKK FOR SETUP (ACTUAL) |
|---|---|---|---|---|
| I | $A_1$ | 4 | **45** | **4,950** |
| | $A_2$ | 2 | **26** | **2,860** |
| | $A_3$ | 1 | **15** | **1,500** |
| | $B_1$ | 5 | **43** | **4,816** |
| | $B_2$ | 0 | **0** | **0** |
| | total | 12 | 129 | 14,126 |
| | average/setup | | 10.75 | 1,177.2 |
| | average/hour | | | 109.5 |
| II | $A_1$ | 8 | **50** | **3,900** |
| | $A_2$ | 10 | **78** | **6,300** |
| | $A_3$ | 7 | **74** | **5,900** |
| | $B_1$ | 15 | **88** | **7,120** |
| | $B_2$ | 9 | **68** | **5,310** |
| | total | 49 | 358 | 28,530 |
| | average/setup | | 7.31 | 582.2 |
| | average/hour | | | 79.7 |
| BOTH | total | 61 | 487 | 42,656 |
| | average/setup | | 7.98 | 699.3 |
| | average/hour | | | 87.6 |

Note: Further depth of registration could be achieved by associating the number of hours of each setup action with each combination of machine class/product, plus by measuring the costs consumption of each.

Table 1 shows an example of a depth of registration corresponding to figure 11b. It is worth noting, however, that only the figures in bold type would be recorded in a variability accounting system corresponding to this depth. The other figures are merely calculations carried out on this basis.

The table will be used to illustrate the two-stage allocation procedure used by Cooper for the allocation of setup costs. The registrations needed for this purpose are shown in the table as underlined figures.

**Calculation**

*First-stage allocation base*:
The number of setup hours used on machine class I and II respectively are used for the allocation of the total setup costs of the two machine classes. We therefore get the following setup costs in the two ACP's for setup, designated ACP I and ACP II respectively:

ACP I : 129 setup hours @ DKK 87.6/setup hour = DKK 11,299
ACP II: 358 setup hours @ DKK 87.6/setup hour = DKK 31,357

*Second-stage allocation base, Cost Driver*:
The number of setups per product on individual machines is used as a driver for the cost consumption of setup. Setup costs per setup differentiated according to machine class are therefore:

Costs per setup, machine class I : DKK 11,299 ÷ 12 = DKK 941.6/setup
Costs per setup, machine class II: DKK 31,357 ÷ 49 = DKK 639.9/setup

The ex post result calculated for setup costs per product/machine class can subsequently be stated as in table 2 below.

As described in chapter 2.1, Cooper sets the limitation on the allocation base which allocates setup costs to the products that at each stage – first-stage allocation base and second-stage driver – an identical amount per unit of the respective allocation bases must be allocated. Since we are talking about *allocations* here, as opposed to measurements, it is my contention that this is an unnecessary limitation.

Assume, for example, that plan data on setup time and consumption of other setup resources reveal differences as a function of both machine class and product. Even if we have such data at our disposal, but regard the cost of information gathering as too excessive at this level of specification, it is still possible to use them as a link in the allocation of costs.

**Table 2**: Result of the allocation of setup costs, with "setup hours" and "number of setups" as first-stage allocation base and second-stage driver respectively. Period X.

| MACHINE CLASS | PRODUCTS | NO. OF SETUPS | TOTAL DKK FOR SETUP (CALCULATED) | TOTAL DKK FOR SETUP (ACTUAL) | DIFF. IN % OF ACTUAL |
|---|---|---|---|---|---|
| I | $A_1$ | 4 | 3,766 | 4,950 | - 24 |
| | $A_2$ | 2 | 1,883 | 2,860 | - 34 |
| | $A_3$ | 1 | 942 | 1,500 | - 37 |
| | $B_1$ | 5 | 4,708 | 4,816 | - 2 |
| | $B_2$ | 0 | 0 | 0 | – |
| | Total | 12 | 11,299 | 14,126 | \|19\| |
| II | $A_1$ | 8 | 5,120 | 3,900 | 31 |
| | $A_2$ | 10 | 6,399 | 6,300 | 2 |
| | $A_3$ | 7 | 4,480 | 5,900 | - 24 |
| | $B_1$ | 15 | 9,599 | 7,120 | 35 |
| | $B_2$ | 9 | 5,759 | 5,310 | 8 |
| | Total | 49 | 31,357 | 28,530 | \|20\| |

Note: The total percent deviation per machine class is calculated as a simple average of the absolute deviations per product. This form of calculation is also used in the following tables.

Assume that the firm has table 3's plan data available (standard hours and standard costs).

**Table 3:** Plan data of setups as a function of machine class and product.

| PRODUCTS | MACHINE CLASS I | MACHINE CLASS II |
|---|---|---|
| | --------- hours --------- | |
| $A_1$ | 9 | 6 |
| $A_2$ | 12 | 8 |
| $A_3$ | 15 | 10 |
| $B_1$ | 9 | 6 |
| $B_2$ | 12 | 8 |
| | --------- DKK --------- | |
| STANDARD COSTS PER HOUR | 100 | 80 |

Further assume that again we only have historical records at a level of aggregation corresponding to the underlined figures in table 1. On this basis, we can now carry out a variance analysis of setup costs. See table 4.

**Table 4**: Variance analysis of setup costs for period X.

| | MACHINE CLASS I | | | MACHINE CLASS II | | |
|---|---|---|---|---|---|---|
| PRODUCTS | NO. OF SETUPS (ACTUAL) | TOTAL STANDARD HOURS FOR ACTUAL SETUP | TOTAL STANDARD COSTS FOR ACTUAL SETUP | NO. OF SETUPS ACTUAL | TOTAL STANDARD HOURS FOR ACTUAL SETUP | TOTAL STANDARD COSTS FOR ACTUAL SETUP |
| | no. | hours | DKK | no. | hours | DKK |
| $A_1$ | 4 | 36 | 3,600 | 8 | 48 | 3,840 |
| $A_2$ | 2 | 24 | 2,400 | 10 | 80 | 6,400 |
| $A_3$ | 1 | 15 | 1,500 | 7 | 70 | 5,600 |
| $B_1$ | 5 | 45 | 4,500 | 15 | 90 | 7,200 |
| $B_2$ | 0 | – | – | 9 | 72 | 5,760 |
| total | 12 | 120 | 12,000 | 49 | 360 | 28,800 |
| efficiency variance | | 9 | 900 | – | - 2 | - 160 |
| actual, total | | 129 | 12,900 | – | 358 | 28,640 |
| | | | | | DKK 41,540 | |
| spending variance | | | | | 1,116 | |
| total actual costs | | | | | 42,656 | |

If standard costs are compared with the potentially deeper registration shown in table 1, the following result is obtained (table 5).

**Table 5**: Comparison of standard costs and actual costs of setups. Period X.

| | MACHINE CLASS I | | | MACHINE CLASS II | | |
|---|---|---|---|---|---|---|
| PRODUCTS | TOTAL STANDARD COSTS FOR ACTUAL SETUP | TOTAL DKK FOR SETUP (ACTUAL) | DIFF. IN % OF ACTUAL | TOTAL STANDARD COSTS FOR ACTUAL SETUP | TOTAL DKK FOR SETUP (ACTUAL) | DIFF. IN % OF ACTUAL |
| $A_1$ | 3,600 | 4,950 | - 27 | 3,840 | 3,900 | - 2 |
| $A_2$ | 2,400 | 2,860 | - 16 | 6,400 | 6,300 | 2 |
| $A_3$ | 1,500 | 1,500 | 0 | 5,600 | 5,900 | - 5 |
| $B_1$ | 4,500 | 4,816 | - 7 | 7,200 | 7,120 | 1 |
| $B_2$ | – | 0 | – | 5,760 | 5,310 | 8 |
| Total | 12,000 | 14,126 | \|10\| | 28,800 | 28,530 | \|4\| |

If a variance analysis shows an approximately stationary percentage of efficiency- and spending variance over successive accounting periods, with different mixes and scopes of "setups", it is reasonable to assume that standard costs can serve as allocation base for actual setup costs. The result of such a procedure for period X can be seen in table 6. Here, the efficiency- and spending variance percentage is simply allocated against the respective setups, with standard costs as allocation base.

**Table 6**: Allocation of actual costs, with standard costs as allocation base. Period X.

| | MACHINE CLASS I | | | MACHINE CLASS II | | |
|---|---|---|---|---|---|---|
| PRODUCTS | TOTAL COSTS FOR ACTUAL SETUP (CALCULATED) | TOTAL DKK FOR SETUP (ACTUAL) | DIFF. IN % OF ACTUAL | TOTAL COSTS FOR ACTUAL SETUP (CALCULATED) | TOTAL DKK FOR SETUP (ACTUAL) | DIFF. IN % OF ACTUAL |
| $A_1$ | 3,974 | 4,950 | - 20 | 3,921 | 3,900 | - 1 |
| $A_2$ | 2,649 | 2,860 | - 7 | 6,535 | 6,300 | 4 |
| $A_3$ | 1,656 | 1,500 | 10 | 5,718 | 5,900 | - 3 |
| $B_1$ | 4,968 | 4,816 | - 3 | 7,352 | 7,120 | 3 |
| $B_2$ | – | 0 | – | 5,882 | 5,310 | 11 |
| Total | 13,247 | 14,126 | \|8\| | 29,408 | 28,530 | \|4\| |

We can also use this example to illustrate how a greater depth of registration would affect the validity of our description of costs:

Alternatively, if we imagine that we have registered – i.e. directly measured – the cost consumption of "setup" on the two machine classes, but failed at the same time to identify the products for which the "setup" was carried out, then as far as data is concerned, we are still better off than with the basis used in table 2, since we now at least have the two amounts, DKK 14,126 and DKK 28,530. Resource use is registrered in the department which provides the "setup" service. This not only requires the registration of time used on the two machine classes, but also the identification, for each machine class, of other types of costs incurred with "setup". If the receiving department (the department which actually produces the products) has registered the number of batches per product (here equal to the number of setups), then we have sufficient information for table 7:

**Table 7**: Result of cost allocation, excluding the first-stage allocation base, but including the second-stage driver: "number of setups per product". Period X.

| MACHINE CLASS | PRODUCTS | NO. OF SETUPS | TOTAL DKK FOR SETUP (CALCULATED) | TOTAL DKK FOR SETUP (ACTUAL) | DIFF. IN % OF ACTUAL |
|---|---|---|---|---|---|
| I | $A_1$ | 4 | 4,709 | 4,950 | - 5 |
| | $A_2$ | 2 | 2,354 | 2,860 | -18 |
| | $A_3$ | 1 | 1,177 | 1,500 | - 22 |
| | $B_1$ | 5 | 5,886 | 4,816 | 22 |
| | $B_2$ | 0 | 0 | 0 | – |
| | Total | 12 | 14,126 | 14,126 | \|13\| |
| II | $A_1$ | 8 | 4,658 | 3,900 | 19 |
| | $A_2$ | 10 | 5,822 | 6,300 | - 8 |
| | $A_3$ | 7 | 4,076 | 5,900 | - 31 |
| | $B_1$ | 15 | 8,734 | 7,120 | 23 |
| | $B_2$ | 9 | 5,240 | 5,310 | - 1 |
| | Total | 49 | 28,530 | 28,530 | \|16\| |

If, in addition, the "setup" department has registered the consumption of time by product type, then we can present the tabulation as in table 8. The only thing we need, in relation to the deepest form of registration dealt with in table

1, is an identification of the other "setup" costs per product. Compared with actual consumption, the differences in the example are negligible.

**Table 8**: Result of cost allocation, excluding the first-stage allocation base, but including the second-stage driver: "setup hours per product". Period X.

| MACHINE CLASS | PRODUCTS | NO. OF SETUPS | TOTAL DKK FOR SETUP (CALCULATED) | TOTAL DKK FOR SETUP (ACTUAL) | DIFF. IN % OF ACTUAL |
|---|---|---|---|---|---|
| I | $A_1$ | 45 | 4,928 | 4,950 | - 0 |
| | $A_2$ | 26 | 2,847 | 2,860 | - 0 |
| | $A_3$ | 15 | 1,643 | 1,500 | - 10 |
| | $B_1$ | 43 | 4,816 | 4,816 | 2 |
| | $B_2$ | 0 | 0 | 0 | – |
| | Total | 129 | 14,127 | 14,126 | \|2\| |
| II | $A_1$ | 50 | 3,985 | 3,900 | 2 |
| | $A_2$ | 78 | 6,216 | 6,300 | - 1 |
| | $A_3$ | 74 | 5,897 | 5,900 | - 0 |
| | $B_1$ | 88 | 7,013 | 7,120 | 2 |
| | $B_2$ | 68 | 5,419 | 5,310 | 2 |
| | Total | 358 | 28,530 | 28,530 | \|1\| |

**Supplement 1**

# General Account Code of Variability Accounting

| CLASS 6 TYPES OF PRODUCTION FACTORS | CLASS 7 DEPARTMENTS | CLASS 8 OBJECTIVES |
|---|---|---|
| 60 consumption of inventory materials | 70 management of the company as a whole with staff and secretariat | 80 common objectives |
| 61 consumption of non-inventory materials | 71 finance, planning and purchasing departments | 81 administrative objectives |
| 62 wages and other costs of blue-collar workers | 72 research and development department | 82 product development objectives |
| 63 salaries and other costs of white-collar workers | 73 construction department | 83 product manufacturing objectives |
| 64 external services | 74 production departments | 84 repair and maintenance objectives |
| 65 cost reductions | 75 transport department | 85 distribution objectives |
| | 76 various internal service departments | 86 various internal service objectives |
| | 77 sales department | 87 sales objectives |
| | 78 sales service department | 88 sales service objectives |
| 69 balancing with financial accounts | 79 advertising department | 89 advertising objectives |

Source: Vagn Madsen, *Budgettering*, Copenhagen, 1970 (my translation)

Note: In his book on budgeting, Vagn Madsen makes a distinction between "operating objectives" and "investment objectives". This distinction is not included here, since it is primarily concerned with the treatment of costs in the financial statements - not least in the question of capitalization in the balance sheet or immediately written off in the profit & loss statement. The "investment objectives" include, e.g. "in-house construction of major buildings and equipment", "major repairs", and costs associated with establishing major "administrative-", "product development-", and "(other) intangible assets".

**Supplement 2**

# Examples of Recording in the Variability Accounting System

This supplement includes two of Vagn Madsen's figures – here called figure A and B.

*Note to figure A:*
If we examine the figure more closely, viewing the first column as an objectives dimension, then we would have to admit – which Vagn Madsen's figure also indicates – that the product dimension *can be* important in explaining and predicting the development in these cost objectives. In our interpretation of variability accounting, any interaction there may be between administrative services and products is handled via the choice of load factor units.

For example: If the resource input in "inspections" (cf. figure) is dependent on the type of product being inspected, then we cannot use "number of inspections" as the load factor unit, but have to use "number of inspections of product-type 1", "number of inspections of product-type 2", etc. To arrive at the budget costs – or to be able to analyse the costs embodied in the ex post accounts – of "inspections", we would thus have to convert from product-specific load factor units to a common capacity utilization unit (presumably expressed in hours).

*Note to figure B:*
The arrows in the figure indicate that, on account of the difficulties, or costs of recording, costs are recorded against the "superjacent account", even though they have a variability-like connection to the "subjacent account".

**Figure A**: Example of administration costs in the production departments.

| | | Production departments | | | Administrative departments | | | | Product types | | | |
|---|---|---|---|---|---|---|---|---|---|---|---|---|
| | Total | A | B | C | P | D | W | O | 1 | 2 | 3 | 0 |
| *Pre-production phase:* | | | | | | | | | | | | |
| – Receive order from planning dept. . . . . . . . . . | | – | – | – | – | | | | – | – | – | |
| – Make changes and additions to specifications, plus discussions with design department . . . | | – | – | – | | – | | | – | – | – | |
| – Detailed planning and paperwork prior to passing the order down to shop floor in the form of work notes . . . . . . | | – | – | – | – | | | | – | – | – | |
| – Dealing with wrong dispositions of other production depts.: Materials late in arriving, tools dispatched to wrong place, etc. . . . . . . . . . . . . | | – | – | – | | | | – | | | | – |
| *Production phase:* | | | | | | | | | | | | |
| – Employee enquiries and dealing with these . . . . . . | | – | – | – | | – | | | – | – | – | |
| – Inspection . . . . . . . . . . . . | | – | – | – | | – | | | – | – | – | |
| – Dealing with production stoppages . . . . . . . . . . . . . | | – | – | – | | | | – | | | | – |
| *Post-production phase:* | | | | | | | | | | | | |
| – Product inspection . . . . . . | | – | – | – | | – | | | – | – | – | |
| – Work note administration: Signing, correction for scrap, comments . . . . . . . | | – | – | – | – | | | | – | – | – | |
| – Messages to planning dept., warehouse, or next-receiving dept. (covering notes, etc.) . . . . | | – | – | – | – | | | | – | – | – | |
| – Checking of piecework jobs . . . . . . . . . . . . . . . . . | | – | – | – | – | – | – | | – | – | – | |
| *Other:* | | | | | | | | | | | | |
| – Piecework negotiations . . . | | – | – | – | | | – | | – | – | – | |
| – Other employee-related negotiations . . . . . . . . . . . | | – | – | – | | | | – | | | | – |
| – "Slack time", waiting time for foreman . . . . . . . . . . . | | – | – | – | – | | | | | | – | |

Note: P = planning department, D = design department, W = wages department, O = other. It should be noted that, according to Vagn Madsen's accompanying text, the whole of the first column is viewed as a specification of production factor costs (Danish: omkostningsarter), whereas I call them cost objectives.

Source: Vagn Madsen, *Bidrag til Belysning af Rationaliseringsproblemerne i Industrivirksomheder*, Copenhagen, 1951, figure 18, p. 79.

**Figure B**: Example of variability accounting records centring around production batches.

| | | Costs per product part | Costs per batch | Costs per product |
|---|---|---|---|---|
| *Production statistics* | | | | |
| Materials | Consumption of product parts | | | |
| | Cutting Alloys | | ← | |
| | Oil | | ← | |
| | Indirect materials | | ← | |
| | Rejects | | | |
| Work description | Machine setup | | | |
| | Direct work | | | |
| | Transport | | ← | |
| | Control, inspection, testing of tolerances | | ← | |
| Other | Electricity | | ← | |
| | Templates and setup tools | | | ← |
| *Administration-cost statistics in the production departments* | | | | |
| Pre-production phase | Receiving orders from and messages in planning department | | | |
| | Making changes and additions to specifications | | | |
| | Detailed planning of orders (in the form of work notes) | | | ← |
| Production phase | Technical enquiries from employees, and dealing with these | | | |
| | Batch inspection of work in progress | | | ← |
| Post-production phase | Product inspection | | | ← |
| | Recording of work notes | | | ← |
| | Messages to planning dept., warehouse, and /or next dept. (eventual covering notes) | | | ← |
| Other | Piecework negotiations | | | |
| *Design department costs statistics* | | | | |
| | Technical drawings | | | |
| | Tolerance calculations | | | |
| | Working drawings, write out specifications | | | ← |
| | Tests and trials | | | |
| | Checking old drawings | | | |
| | Customer complains reports | | | |
| *Planning department cost statistics* | | | | |
| Planning | Checking specifications | | | ← |
| | Writing out work notes | | | ← |
| | Dealing with rush orders | | | ← |
| Checking | Signing of finished goods | | | ← |
| | | Σ | Σ | |

Note: The whole of the first column is, in Vagn Madsen's accompanying text, viewed as a specification of production factor costs (Danish: omkostningsarter), whereas I call them cost objectives.

Source: Vagn Madsen: *Bidrag til Belysning af Rationaliseringsproblemerne i Industrivirksomheder,* fig 39, p. 117.

**Supplement 3**

# Example of an Inspiration Analysis[1]

Figure X shows a stylised example of the departments and flow of goods of a complex firm. This complexity is partly hidden in the figure because the flow of finished products only shows product lines, not single products. In reality, there are numerous variants in each line. Assume also that all four product lines are manufactured on the same machinery, and that lines A, B, and D are standard products, while product line C consists of customer adapted specialized products.

**Figure X**: Some departments and a product flow

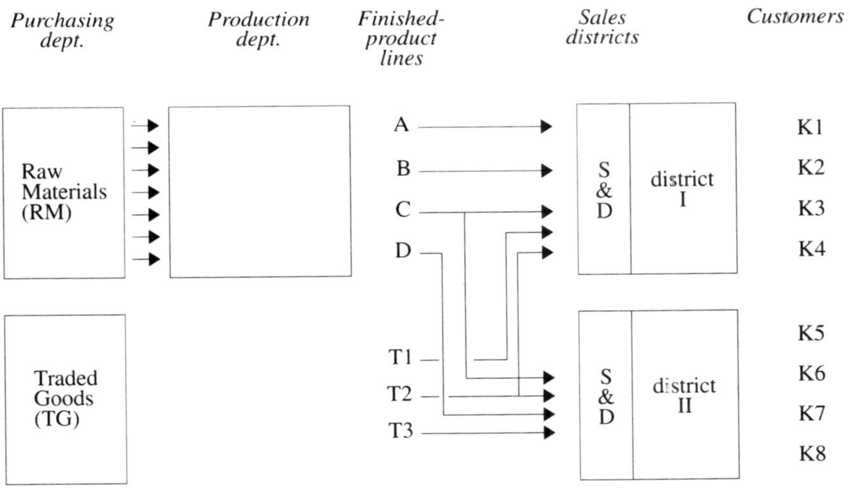


1. Source: Israelsen & Sørensen: Nye økonomistyringsudfordringer, *FSR's Årsskrift*, FSR's Forlag, 1991, pp. 110-115. (My translation). Reproduced by permission of co-author and publisher.

Figures Y and Z show two contribution margin layouts which follow the stepped contribution margin principle. Figure Y focuses on an analysis of products, while figure Z analyses customers and sales districts.

**Figure Y**: Stepped Contribution Margin Layout, showing Contribution Margin (CM) per Product as Intermediate Results – Year X.

| *Product Lines* | **A** | **B** | **C** | **D** | **T1** | **T2** | **T3** |
|---|---|---|---|---|---|---|---|
| Gross Revenue<br>– commission on sales<br>– discount per unit | | | | | | | |
| Net Revenue<br>– production-direct variable costs | | | | | | | |
| CM per product | CMA | CMB | CMC | CMD | CMT1 | CMT2 | CMT3 |
| CM Produced in-house | | a | | | | | |
| CM Traded goods | | | | | | b | |
| – Single-period capacity costs:<br>*– in Production & RM Purchasing Depts.* | | c | | | | | |
| *– in TG Purchasing Dept.* | | | | | | d | |
| Gross Profit Margin (GPM) per product group | | e | | | | f | |
| GPM, pre-distribution | | | | g | | | |
| *– Single-period capacity costs in Sales & Distribution (S&D)* | | | | h | | | |
| GPM, pre-depreciation | | | | GPM | | | |

Note: This layout format is especially pertinent in analysing the contribution which traded goods make to the firm. A negative intermediate result at the "f" level, for example, would signal the need for selective marketing measures here.

If we assume a very high degree of reliability in the cost allocation (a number of operator wages are not even product-direct), then we must expect that, on the basis of figure Y, the average contribution margin ratio for in-house

**Figure Z**: Stepped Contribution Margin Layout, showing Contribution per Customer and per District as Intermediate Results – Year X.

| *Customer/Customer Groups* | **K1** | **K2** | **K3** | **K4** | **K5** | **K6** | **K7** | **K8** |
|---|---|---|---|---|---|---|---|---|
| Gross Revenue | | | | | | | | |
| – commission on sales | | | | | | | | |
| – discount per unit | | | | | | | | |
| – other customer-direct variable costs | | | | | | | | |
| Net Revenue | | | | | | | | |
| – production-direct variable costs | | | | | | | | |
| CM per Customer | CMK1 | CMK2 | CMK3 | CMK4 | CMK5 | CMK6 | CMK7 | CMK8 |
| CM District I | | A | | | | | | |
| CM District II | | | | | | B | | |
| – Single-period Capicity costs: | | | | | | | | |
| *– in S&D / district I* | | C | | | | | | |
| *– in S&D / district II* | | | | | | D | | |
| CM per district | | E | | | | F | | |
| Gross Profit Margin (GPM) before Capacity Cost in Production and Purchasing | | | | G | | | | |
| – Single-period Capacity Costs: | | | | | | | | |
| *– in Production Dept.* | | | | H | | | | |
| *– in Purchasing (RM+TG)* | | | | I | | | | |
| *– Other* | | | | J | | | | |
| GPM, pre-depreciation | | | | GPM | | | | |

Note: This layout format is especially relevant for economic analyses of customers and districts.

products is markedly higher than for traded goods. We must also expect a higher contribution margin for the C line than for the other in-house products. In the absence of any capacity limitations on production equipment, product-line C would therefore be a strong contender for expansion. Even more so if its products show the highest contribution margin per unit of capacity (including the time consumed in setup of the equipment) on the production capacity which would be the first to become scarce with continuing expansion.

If we assume that product line C is sold to all customer groups, but primarily to group K2, then in the figure Z layout, this customer/customer group will show the highest contribution margin ratio per customer/group. Both types of analysis thus show – with a high degree of reliability in the contribution margin calculations – that product line C and customer K2 are economically profitable segments.

Return to figure Y for a moment, and imagine that an important item under the single-period production capacity costs is engineer-salaries in component- and product design on the C line. Now if the driver or capacity utilization measure, which describes the load factor hereof, is "number of blueprints" or "number of design hours", we could use this base to allocate these costs among the four in-house product lines. This allocation base is *not* arbitrary, *which would otherwise be the case with the use of "direct materials value" or "machine hours"*, for example. The allocated costs *are* arbitrary, however, since no account has been taken of the production factor's absolute and relative divisibility in the allocation concerned.

If we assume that, as a result of this allocation[2], a percentage calculation of gross profit leaves line C lower down the order of precedence of in-house products than a gross contribution margin ratio comparison would, then it is now less obvious that this line should unreservedly be expanded.

Likewise, we could take a closer look at the single-period capacity costs in sales and distributions (S&D) in figure Z. An analysis could result in the assessment that a considerable portion of the costs of order-handling is due to "number of sales orders". If this driver (capacity utilization measure) is used to allocate the activity costs of sales-order handling among customers, and if K2's annual turnover is made up of a relatively large number of orders, then this alone will lead to a reduction in the relative profitability of K2.

Finally, if we assume that, taken in isolation, neither allocation (design costs and sales-order costs) shows the C line and customer/customer group K2 to be loss-making – or even worse than the other segments in a relative comparison of gross margin ratios, for that matter – it does not rule out their being so if the two allocations are combined. If K2 is loss-making under this scenario,

2. Or after similar treatment of the single-period capacity costs in purchases of raw-material types, where the driver could be "number of raw materials numbers", and under the realistic assumption that line C uses relatively more types of raw materials than the other product lines.

then one is faced with the classic dilemma that the C line and K2 customer group are profitable in the short term, but not in the long term – at least not with existing production methods and pricing policy for the C line and the purchasing behaviour displayed by K2. There is therefore a need for selective production and/or marketing measures.

*One* possible action is the elimination of K2. So far, however, the analysis gives no indication of the economic consequences of such a decision. First of all we need a budgetary forecast of this customer's/customer group's demand, and, in addition, to carry out an actual *discontinuance* calculation. In such a calculation we need to take account of the relative divisibility of the costs assigned to the two activities. It is worth noting that we *also* need to know about the driver/capacity utilization measure in the discontinuance calculation, and, in addition, to assess the service efficiency of the units of capacity – i.e. the number of driver units per capacity unit (technical coefficients) – in order to estimate how many units of capacity can be disposed of.

The discontinuance calculation and the inspiration analysis give different results, not least due to incongruities between capacity units and the difference in the (actual and) budgeted utilization of these units. *An inspiration analysis, however, in which the assignment of capacity costs is based on a non-arbitrary capacity utilization measure is more likely to result in an identification of those segments of the firm in need of a policy adjustments than if the analysis is based on arbitrary allocations – i.e. unit drivers – as well.*

# Bibliography


Beaujon, G.J. & V.R. Singhal: "Understanding the Activity Costs in an Activity-Based Cost System", *Journal of Cost Management,* Spring 1990, pp. 51-72.

Böhm, H. H. & F. Wille: *Deckungsbeitragsrechnung und Optimierung,* 6th edition, Munich, 1977.

Cooper, Robin: "The Rise of Activity-based Costing – Part One: What is an Activity-Based Cost System?", *Journal of Cost Management,* Summer 1988 pp. 45-54.

Cooper, R.: "The Rise of Activity-based Costing – Part Two: When do I Need an Activity-Based Cost System?", *Journal of Cost Management,* Fall 1988, pp. 41-48.

Cooper, R.: "The Rise of Activity-based Costing – Part Three: How many Cost Drivers Do You Need, and How do You Select Them?", *Journal of Cost Management,* Winter 1989, pp. 34-46.

Cooper, R.: "The Rise of Activity-based Costing – Part Four: What Do Activity-Based Cost Systems Look Like?", *Journal of Cost Management,* Spring 1989, pp. 38-49.

Cooper, R.: "Cost Classification in Unit-Based and Activity-Based Manufacturing Cost Systems", *Journal of Cost Management*, Fall 1990, pp. 4-14.

Cooper, R. & Robert S. Kaplan: "How Cost Accounting Distorts Product Costs", *Management Accounting* (NAA), April 1988, pp. 20-27.

Cooper, R. & R.S. Kaplan: "Measure Cost Right: Make the Right Decisions", *Harvard Business Review,* Sept.-Oct. 1988, pp. 96-103.

Cooper, R. & R.S. Kaplan: *Activity-Based Profitability Analysis*, February, 1990, (Draft manuscript, 23 pages).

Cooper, R. & R.S. Kaplan: *THE DESIGN OF COST MANAGEMENT SYSTEMS, Text, Cases, and Readings*, Englewood Cliffs, New Jersey, 1991.

Cooper, R & R.S. Kaplan: "Profit Priorities from Activity-Based Costing", *Harvard Business Review,* May-June, 1991, pp. 130-135.

Israelsen, Poul: "Lader Vagn Madsens og Zakken Worres tanker og ideer omkring virksomhedens omkostningsregnskab sig forene? in Nørreklit, L. *et al.*: Aktuelle Forskningsprojekter I og Omkring Revision, *Faglige Artikler 23*, Foreningen af Yngre Revisorer, Copenhagen, 1989, pp. 179-208.

Israelsen, P. & P.E. Sørensen: "Nye Økonomistyringsudfordringer" in Ole Øhlenschlæger Madsen & Andreas Nicolaisen (eds.), *Revision og Erhvervsøkonomi, FSR's Årsskrift 1991*, pp. 69-125.

Johnson, H. T. & R.S. Kaplan: *RELEVANCE LOST: The Rise and Fall of Management Accounting,* Harvard Business School Press, 1987.

Johnson, H. T.: "Activity-Based Information: A Blueprint for World-Class Management Accounting", *Management Accounting* (NAA), June 1988, pp. 23-30.

Kaplan, R. S.: "The Evolution of Management Accounting", *Accounting Review,* Vol. LIX, No. 3, July 1984, pp. 390-418.

Kaplan, R. S.: "Yesterday's Accounting Undermines Production", *Harvard Business Review,* July-August 1984. pp. 95-101.

Kaplan, R. S.: "Accounting Lag: The Obsolescence of Cost Accounting Systems", *California Management Review,* Vol. XXVIII, Number 2, Winter 1986, pp. 174-199.

Kaplan, R. S.: "One Cost System Isn't Enough", *Harvard Business Review,* January-February, 1988, pp. 61-66.

Kilger, Wolfgang: *Flexible Plankostenrechnung und Deckungsbeitragsrechnung*, 9th edition, Wiesbaden, 1988.

King, Alfred M. "The Current Status of Activity-Based Costing: An interview with Robin Cooper and Robert S. Kaplan", *Management Accounting* (NAA), September, 1991, pp. 22-26.

Madsen, Vagn: *Bidrag til Belysning af Rationaliseringsproblemerne i Industrivirksomheder,* Copenhagen, 1951.

Madsen, V.: *Budgettering,* Copenhagen, 1970.

Madsen, V.: *Regnskabsvæsenets opgaver og problemer – i ny belysning,* 2. edition, Copenhagen, 1969.

Madsen, V.: *Strategi og budget,* Copenhagen, 1976.

Madsen, V. & T. Polesie: *Human Factors in Budgeting: Judgement and Evaluation,* Pitman Press, London, 1981.

Nanni, A. J., J.G. Miller & T.E. Vollmann: "What Shall We Account For?", *Management Accounting* (NNA), January 1988, pp. 42-48.

Polesie, T.: *Ändamålsbudgettering – beskrivning och analys af tillämpninger,* Studentlitteratur, Lund, 1976.

Riebel, Paul: *Einzelkosten- und Deckungsbeitragsrechnung,* 6th thoroughly enlarged edition, Wiesbaden, 1990.

Robinson, Michael A. (ed.): "Contribution Margin Analysis: No Longer Relevant/Strategic Cost Management: The New Paradigm", *Journal of Management Accounting Research,* Fall 1990, pp. 1-32.

Rørsted, Bent: *Balance Lost – An Appraisal of Activity-Based Costing*, IFV, Aarhus University, 1990.

Rørsted, B.: *Activity-Based Confusion? – ABC-status primo 1991*, IFV, Aarhus University, 1991.

Rørsted, B.: Activity-Based Costing 1987-1991, *Revision og Regnskabsvæsen*, no. 10, 1991.

Simon, H. A.: *Administrative Behavior,* The Macmillan Comp., N.Y., 1961.

Sørensen, P. E.: "Indledende betragtninger over behovet for et ændret omkostningsregistreringsbegreb" in Nørreklit, L. *et al.*: Aktuelle Forskningsprojekter I og Omkring Revision, *Faglige Artikler 23*, Foreningen af Yngre Revisorer, Copenhagen, 1989, pp. 209-220.

Umble, M.M. & M.L. Srikanth: *Synchronous Manufacturing*, Cincinnati, Ohio, 1990.

Worre, Zakken: *Noter til internt regnskabsvæsen*, Copenhagen, 1973.

Worre, Z.: *Registrering og styring af kapacitetsomkostninger*, Copenhagen, 1991.

Worre, Z.: *Omkostningsregnskab og Omkostningsstyring – Omkostningsregnskabets begreber samt regnskabet med vareforbrug, materialer og arbejdsløn*, Volume 1, Copenhagen, 1991.

Worre, Z.: *Omkostningsregnskab og Omkostningsstyring – Udvikling og demonstration af en generel registrerings- og styringsmodel for kapacitetsomkostninger og salgsindsats*, Volume 2, Copenhagen, 1991.

# Index